The Middle Ages: A Very Short Introduction

VERY SHORT INTRODUCTIONS are for anyone wanting a stimulating and accessible way in to a new subject. They are written by experts, and have been translated into more than 40 different languages.

The Series began in 1995, and now covers a wide variety of topics in every discipline. The VSI library now contains over 350 volumes—a Very Short Introduction to everything from Psychology and Philosophy of Science to American History and Relativity—and continues to grow in every subject area.

Very Short Introductions available now:

Available soon:

For more information visit our website
www.oup.com/vsi/

Miri Rubin

THE MIDDLE AGES

A Very Short Introduction

OXFORD
UNIVERSITY PRESS

Great Clarendon Street, Oxford, OX2 6DP,
United Kingdom

Oxford University Press is a department of the University of Oxford.
It furthers the University's objective of excellence in research, scholarship,
and education by publishing worldwide. Oxford is a registered trade mark of
Oxford University Press in the UK and in certain other countries

© Miri Rubin 2014

The moral rights of the author have been asserted

First edition published in 2014

Published in the United States of America by Oxford University Press
198 Madison Avenue, New York, NY 10016, United States of America

British Library Cataloguing in Publication Data
Data available

Library of Congress Control Number: 2014939949

ISBN 978-0-19-969729-8

Printed and bound by CPI Group (UK) Ltd, Croydon, CR0 4YY

Contents

Acknowledgements

An invitation to write a *Very Short Introduction* is an honour and an opportunity. It is also a daunting task. Much of what I have learned from historians past and present has gone into the making of this book, as have insights gained in answer to students' questions. Oxford University Press asked five experts to judge the proposal, and two colleagues read the final draft: I am full of appreciation for the advice of these anonymous collaborators. Several generous friends provided useful opinions, crucial information, and a few even commented on the whole text with critical insight and encouragement. Among them are Matthew Champion, Peter Denley, Emma Dillon, Yaniv Fox, Yitzhak Hen, Eyal Poleg, Magnus Ryan, Chris Sparks, Gareth Stedman Jones, David Wallace, and Simon Yarrow.

I am most grateful to the dynamic team at Oxford University Press—led by Emma Ma—for their guidance and professional support, and to Dorothy McCarthy who worked on the final text so carefully.

I dedicate this book to my dear friend and historian extraordinaire, Shulamith Shahar.

List of illustrations

List of maps

Introduction

This *Very Short Introduction* will offer two approaches to a fruitful engagement with the long period of European history known as the Middle Ages, ranging from around 500 to around 1500.

The term Middle Ages—the French *Moyen Âge* or the Italian *medioevo*—speaks of a sole 'Age', and this is misleading. The concept of an 'age' fails to capture the fact that we are dealing with a vast territory over a long period in constant transformation. As we explore continuity and change we will find that Europe did not live to a single rhythm over this period. While there was vibrant city life in Italy, Iberia, and southern France from early in the period, substantial urban centres and commerce developed in England and France only in the 12th century, in Bohemia in the 13th, and in the Baltic regions only in the 14th. Similarly, Europe's regions became Christian at different times: Rome with its ancient Christian communities, the Franks from *c*.500, Iceland *c*.1000, and Livonia in the Baltic region, in the 1300s. If we think of religious change, then the parish system reached most Europeans after 1200; if the rhythms of agrarian life are considered, then many aspects of our period remained in place until the 18th century.

As we shall see, during our period several cultures and peoples came into contact—always learning from each other; they sometimes clashed, and ultimately blended. There was the heritage of the Roman Empire with its city life, its Christian intellectual heritage, its concept of citizenship, its trade, and its principles of election to public office in service of the common good—*res publica*. And there was the growing influence of the values and capacities of the kin-based societies of the Germanic peoples—barbarians, to medieval people 'bearded ones'—who at the beginning of our period were already long-standing neighbours and even members of the Roman Empire. Add to that the impact of the spread of Islam in the Mediterranean countries from the 7th century, and the role played by Islamic Europe in shaping politics and disseminating whole areas of knowledge, and our period emerges in its complexity. As these forces were at play European lives were shaped through all manner of human exchange and interaction: conquest, conversion, imitation, legislation, and persuasion.

Even the word Europe is far from fixed. I shall use it to describe the westernmost part of a vast continental mass, an area in which a shared Christian culture came to prevail among an ever growing group of polities and their people, and whose genealogy is linked to the later Roman Empire. Its kingdoms and peoples formed an interlocking commonwealth based on an integrated economy, a universal framework for religious life, with an intellectual elite that communicated in Latin, and a secular elite bound by marriage, diplomacy, war, and lifestyle.

Europe's people and places interest us above all. Since the early-20th century historians have sought to make history more inclusive, to reach people and phenomena largely ignored by previous historians. French historian Marc Bloch (1886–1944) has taught us how to study agrarian societies in their great variety and dynamism; Jacques Le Goff (1924–2014) showed how rich was the intellectual and commercial life of cities. In their wake many other historians have helped make these centuries of European history diverse and challenging. Alongside kings and queens, bishops and nobles we now consider intellectuals and peasants, merchants and women, Jews and nuns. We also attend to the materials they used and the shape and sounds of their environments. From these arise norms and transgressions, continuity and change, the constraints and vulnerabilities of people's lives, alongside opportunity and aspiration.

If you are about to study history at university, or have become interested in the European past through travel, film, or fantasy literature, then you will have come across the term Middle Ages; hence we use it here. But we should not do so without testing its origins and assumption. That is how we will begin this *Very Short Introduction.*

Chapter 1
The 'Middle' Ages?

The 'Middle' Ages: what's in a name?

Like many European concepts the Middle Ages is one which
eventually reached all parts of the world, shaping how people
think about Europe and its people. The 'Middle Ages' is in reality
an awkward term with which to explore the centuries between
500 and 1500. It suggests that this was a time of arrested
motion, a time between two other important epochs that define
its middle-ness.

Those who coined the term Middle Ages possessed a tremendous
sense of their own worth and good fortune as members of a later
age. *Media aetas*, that is, Middle Age—was first used by the poet
Petrarch (1304–74), followed in the next century by statesmen and
historians like Leonardo Bruni (*c.*1370–1444) and Flavio Biondi
(1392–1463). These were men of politics and letters who fostered
a style consciously engaged with the study of classical texts and
ideas, with humanism, as they called it. They celebrated their
times and their cities, and above all each other.

Leaders, preachers, and public intellectuals often announce the
dawning of a new age. These are not idle statements, but nor are
they claims that historians need accept at face value. Humanists
like Bruni were proclaiming a particular style of Italian civic

living, which enabled artists, poets, architects, and history-writers to refine their skills within courts and cities, with Tuscany as their epicentre. They were privileged communicators of the cultural treasure that had been Rome's, a culture lost—so they claimed—with the demise of Roman institutions, often marked by the removal of the last western Roman emperor in 476.

Such men came to be known as humanists, intrepid raiders of the treasures of antiquity, hitherto obscured to generations of people living in the 'Middle Age'. This self-awareness—which they were able to express thanks to the patronage they received from princes, popes, and noble families—was displayed with bravura in the poetry and letters they wrote to classical rhythms, and within palaces inspired by the buildings of ancient Rome. When the first history of the period's great artists was written by Giorgio Vasari (1511–74), he saw the rebirth of classical standards as a welcome change after the 'Gothic' age with its soaring pinnacles and pointed arches (Box 1).

Box 1 The Gothic style

The Gothic style in architecture is one of the most enduring inventions of our period. It emerged c.1140 in France—at the abbey of St Denis, at Chartres and Sens cathedrals—and over the subsequent decades spread throughout the whole of Europe. It is a style which values great height and the sense of loftiness, its builders sought to embed large sections of windows in walls, and thus to let in light, beautifully coloured by the tinted glass. The Gothic building was like a canvas for sculpted, painted, and glazed decoration: and all this height and light was meant to inspire and lift the viewer towards contemplating divine things. The Gothic style spread through the work of French artists, in Westminster Abbey in London, and in St Vitus' cathedral in Prague, but many regions—from Sweden to Cyprus—created their own versions.

The Gothic also influenced secular buildings: castles, palaces, and town halls, like the magnificent town hall of Brussels. Italy alone, with its powerful classical tradition and its distinctive local political cultures, was able to resist the allure of the Gothic.

The humanists sensed they were witnesses to the rebirth— *rinascimento*—of classical ideas and practices that had been corrupted during the middling period. Hence the term Renaissance, used since to describe their passionate interests in the culture of antiquity. The men who coined 'Renaissance' were also convinced that Italy was unique in the excellence of its scholars. In reality scholars and readers from all over Europe participated in the Italian literary culture, widely available thanks to the recently invented print.

So let us set aside the 'Middle Ages' and 'Renaissance' as historically descriptive terms, and note the recurring utility of the 'Middle Ages' as a point of reference for people and places in different times.

Medievalism

The way we think about Europe between 500 and 1500 is not only marked by the terms 'Middle Ages' and 'Renaissance'. It is also influenced by the availability across the globe of traces of later revivals, appropriations, and introductions of aspects of the 'medieval' into public life. The aesthetic values of pre-modern Europe were appreciated in a particularly intense manner in the 19th century. This was for some a reaction against the 18th century Enlightenment whose thinkers emphasized the importance of reason in guiding human affairs, and considered earlier times as 'barbarous adventures under barbarous names'. 19th century medievalism sought in that past the values of community—before the rise of commercial society and the global markets—and of spirituality, guided by religious faith. Those who opposed the French Revolution and its bloody aftermath often celebrated the qualities of the old European order, the *ancien régime*—traditional monarchy and established church—as enduring forms of European life, to be cherished—in England or Prussia—or restored, in France.

Madame de Staël (1766–1817), a romantic novelist and commentator on the French Revolution, celebrated the Germanic roots of European civilization in the aesthetic of the Middle Ages. Similarly, historian Thomas Carlyle (1795–1881), in his *Past and Present* of 1843, advocated a new post-Christian 'gospel of work', inspired by what he perceived as the ethos of cooperation and labour in medieval monasteries. In the decades which saw the explosion of industry and the coming of railways to large parts of Europe, and with them both opportunity and human misery, the medieval past offered an image of a world lost, a more manageable society which lived at a humane pace and on a more human scale. The designer and social thinker William Morris (1834–96) sought to capture the qualities of craft labour in his emulation of medieval carving and painting. His was not a yearning for Catholic religion, but for village life, where granaries were the true cathedrals of the people.

There was a notable revival in Catholic activism and building throughout Europe too. When liberal constitutions and reforms removed centuries-old limitations from Catholic citizens, as in England with the Emancipation Act of 1829, new cultural forces came into play. And so, a Catholic convert like Augustus Pugin (1812–52), son of a French émigré, had his hands full with commissions for Catholic cathedrals, chapels, and seminaries in England, Ireland, and even as far as Australia. The Oxford Movement combined the enthusiasm for medieval values with a call for religious reform and the introduction of rituals that the Reformation had dismantled. In France, Catholic worship, abolished during the French Revolution of 1789, was soon restored. Subsequently, the French state sought not to destroy the ancient Catholic heritage but to restore it as part of the nation's history. Large projects financed by the state rebuilt—and often embellished—'Gothic' buildings, most famously the cathedral of Notre Dame in Paris, with its pinnacles, statues, and gargoyles.

Medieval revival was not only a reaction against republican or democratic politics, or the product of Catholic patronage. It also echoed the desires of those who fostered national identities and their expression in nation-states. Nations were understood as being bound by language, history, and landscape, and intellectuals associated with what has been called romantic nationalism—in Germany, Poland, Hungary, or Norway—sought the roots for 19th century national identities in the past. Composer Richard Wagner (1813–83) identified the essence of Germanness in the ancient heroic narratives, which were turned into a poetic cycle in the late-12th century, the *Nibelungenlied*. In France, the architect and conserver Eugène Viollet le Duc (1814–79) led the preservation of medieval abbeys and cathedrals destroyed during the Revolution as part of a national heritage, for every nation needed a clear sense of its past. The novels of Walter Scott (1771–1832) were widely known throughout Europe; they used medieval settings as a frame for the exploration of courage, ingenuity, and ideals of chivalric masculinity. In England, the present was seen as linked to an Anglo-Saxon past through an unbroken tradition of law and nationhood. When the design for rebuilding the Houses of Parliament was sought through public competition in 1836, the Gothic vision of Pugin triumphed, inside and out. The legislative home of English democracy in an age of reform and industry was associated with the age of Magna Carta (1215). In the 20th century an imagined rural Middle Ages of the 'shire' inspired the works of J. R. R. Tolkien (1892–1973)—a professor of medieval English literature—while C. S. Lewis (1898–1963) explored Catholic and medieval themes in his allegorical works, which have become children's classics also loved by adults.

For all these reasons the 'Middle Ages' form a point of reference from which we moderns fashion our identities and conduct our polemics. Hence the many complexions it can assume: the 'medieval' has been associated in turn with socialism and arch-conservatism, with the cohesion of trades unions and the bombast of royal ceremony. The medieval can serve to animate the identity of oppressed minorities, but also the fantasies of expansion and empire-building. It is a legacy and an opportunity; it offers inspiring examples alongside ones to be avoided at all cost. The Middle Ages is always with us—in the design of our cities, in the treasures of our museums, in music, fantasy games, literature, landscape.

Rome and its afterlife

The achievements of the 15th century, so celebrated by humanists, were the continuation of a much longer tradition, which led Europeans to confront—sometimes to reject and often to emulate—the classical cultures of Greece and Rome (Map 1). Antiquity gave rise to diverse religions, philosophies, styles in art and governance, in republics and empires. And between roughly 500 and 1500 this intellectual heritage was explored through reading, copying, and commentary. As they probed that heritage Europeans also imprinted their own stamp upon Latin poetry and prose, Greek medicine and political theory, and on music and architecture too. All spheres of European life—law, theology, political thought, care of the body, religious rituals, and even land tenure—were imprinted by a Roman lore appropriated to varying degrees of imitation and adaptation.

A living classical tradition endured above all in the spheres of governance and religion. The late antique Roman Empire was a Christian polity. This resulted from the process launched by

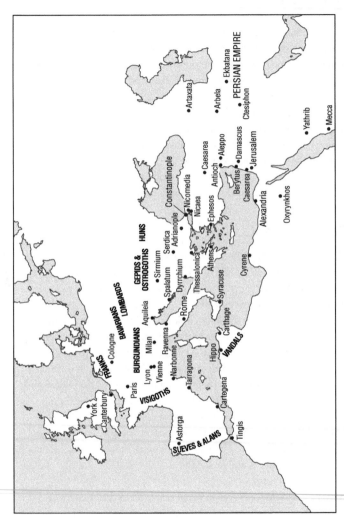

Map 1. Europe c.450

Emperor Constantine (272–337), who embraced Christianity in 312 and made the religion licit within the Empire. Those who followed embedded Christianity into imperial life until it became the official religion by the end of the 4th century.

Contact with ethnic groups at and near its borders had always been a feature of the dynamic Roman Empire. Erstwhile neighbours, indeed enemies, ultimately joined the Roman world; some even became emperors in the 2nd and 3rd centuries. During the 5th century Germanic groups—like the Goths in 418 or the Burgundians in 443—were accommodated with billeting rights, or allocated land for settlement, and sometimes shares in tax revenue. At the beginning of our period the traditional Roman elite—patrician and senatorial families, owners of estates, and stakeholders in Roman political and economic achievements—continued to serve under Germanic rulers. They were educated in the curriculum of the Arts, a rigorous education in logic, composition, and public speaking, alongside training in computation and science. They brought these skills to the important offices of bishops and governors.

From the end of the 3rd century the Roman Empire was in fact managed as two large and interconnected entities: east and west. The western part saw in 476 the deposition of the last Roman emperor Romulus Augustus, by a military leader Odoacer (433–493), who led a federation of Germanic people, and who thus became king of Italy. This change is often used to mark the 'end' of the Roman Empire. It is, in fact, but a stage in the long process by which Germanic groups were incorporated into the Roman armies, garrisoned its borders, settled on state lands, and ultimately also claimed political rule. Odoacer was soon replaced by Theodoric (454–526), king of the Ostrogoths, as ruler of Italy. In 497 Emperor Anastasius—ruler of the Empire from Constantinople—recognized Theodoric and sent to him the regalia of office. Theodoric built his capital in Ravenna as a new

Rome. He appointed court poets who could celebrate his achievements in the Roman imperial style, and maintained the circulation of Roman gold coins. He saw himself as a Christian king—loyal to the Arian branch of Christianity which Constantinople considered a heresy—within a Roman tradition. Similarly, after Clovis, king of the Franks, converted to Christianity in 496, and established regional hegemony by defeating the Visigoths in 508, he too received the Roman title of consul from the same emperor. Through diplomatic contacts with Constantinople, and interaction with local Roman elites, barbarian kings learned how to rule in Roman style.

A Roman civic culture had for centuries animated life in the imperial provinces. Vast investments were made from the imperial coffers in public works and military defences. When these declined in the 4th and 5th centuries, so did the number of city dwellers in Italy, Gaul, and Spain. But the teaching of Latin continued, as did the training of public servants from among the traditional elite of senatorial families. Roman law was practised and people still walked streets laid out in the unmistakable grid of Roman urban planning. Public spaces and practices, like aqueducts, hippodromes, temples, and gladiatorial games were transformed to fit a Christian society. The Pantheon in Rome was turned into a church in 609, dedicated to the Virgin Mary and All Saints.

The kings of the Ostrogoths, Vandals, Franks, Burgundians, and Visigoths were *Roman* barbarians, leaders who cherished what *Romanitas*—Romanness—had to offer. And so, while many have described this period as one of decline and fall of the Roman Empire, a concept popularized by Edward Gibbon (1737–94) in his best-seller *The Decline and Fall of the Roman Empire* (1776), this period of change is better considered as one of *transformation*. That is to say that adaptation rather than destruction characterized the fate of the Roman legacy, and this resulted from intensive—often violent—interaction between peoples.

As the barbarians became Romanized—willingly and alert to the benefits of Roman practices—a hybrid culture emerged. An early-6th century food and health book composed by the Greek physician Anthimus for Theuderic the Great, king of the Franks (c.485–533), subtly acknowledged the Franks' customs while aiming to instil Roman values. Anthimus accepted that high-born barbarians preferred to drink beer and mead—an abomination to any self-respecting Roman—but also recommended the importance of decorum in handling and preparation of food, and consumption of moderate portions. This etiquette stands in contrast to contemporary descriptions—condescending as well as misunderstanding—of barbarian male sociability. Sidonius Apollinaris (430–89), son of a Gallo-Roman senatorial family, diplomat, poet, and then bishop of Clermont, described the Burgundians as reeking of garlic and onion, and as giants who spoke an unintelligible tongue and who groomed their hair with rancid butter.

The continuity of ideas and practices in public administration and economic life was facilitated by the existence of a sole emperor, in Constantinople. Emperor Justinian (c.482–565) attempted to re-establish a sole imperial authority around the Mediterranean—east and west—in regions that for a century had been ruled by Barbarian successor states. He also extended the Empire—now called Byzantium and largely Greek-speaking—eastwards, with triumphs over the Persian Sassanids and the Armenians. His success in battles at sea and on land was matched by ambitious campaigns of construction. Court historian Procopius (c.490–c.560) lovingly describes edifices in Constantinople and in the Holy Land, building projects through which the imprint of the Christian Empire was felt. Even more far-reaching for the lives of individuals and communities were Justinian's legislative efforts: he commissioned a compendium of imperial law, Justinian's *Code*, updating Theodosius II's laws of 438; a *Digest* of learned opinions on questions arising from legal practice; and a law textbook with helpful commentaries, the *Institutions*. Under Justinian

1. **Gold coin minted by Theodebert I (534–48), king of the Franks. Barbarian kings continued to mint such coins, shaped like a Roman *solidus*, as a symbols of authority and economic prosperity**

theological controversies on the nature of Christ animated eastern and western bishops alike as one Christian commonwealth. Soon after, in 568, the Lombard conquest of large parts of northern and central Italy diminished such contacts.

Gold coins now carried the portraits of kings rather than emperors (Figure 1). Coins issued in late 6th century Provence still retained the imperial shape, though they were lighter in weight. Coins facilitated trade in luxury goods that were still available throughout the old Roman provinces, not least in the new royal courts and for ritual use in churches and cathedrals. Coins eased the collection of taxes by a cadre of administrators, officials who still carried Roman titles and who were paid by barbarian kings from the public purse.

The Mediterranean empire that Justinian had sought to revive was soon transformed by the advent of a new force in world history: Islam (Map 2). Born in the Arabian Peninsula, Islam arose from the convergence of diverse traditions, including Judaism and Christianity. It was an exciting new religious ideology which mobilized kinship groups into military action, first in the peninsula and then beyond. The fragmented and battered

Byzantine Empire, which had seen loss of territory and income in the decades following Justinian, offered easy pickings. A decade after the death of Mohammed, in 637, Jerusalem was taken by Caliph Umar, the crowning of his conquest of Byzantine Syria and Palestine. Next he mobilized an army which entered Egypt in 639, and brought it into the fold of the emergent Ummayad Caliphate with its capital in Damascus.

Muslim conquest was led by Arab armies, but these were locally re-inforced by converts to Islam, by defeated Byzantine garrisons, and by alliances with local groups, such as Bedouins in the Sinai, and Berbers in north Africa. These developments soon had dramatic implications for Europeans: the Mediterranean islands, southern France, and Italy suffered from raids and by 711 large parts of Iberia were conquered by a Muslim army from north Africa—led by Tariq ibn Ziyad.

Muslim armies soon crossed the Pyrenees into the Gallic province of Septimania too. Roman-Visigothic cities like Barcelona and Narbonne were taken, but progress deeper into Gaul was halted. This border of Christian/Muslim rule in southwest Europe was held for a generation, until the Franks reclaimed Narbonne in 759. Many of the old Roman provinces now lived under Muslim rule. In Iberia, Visigoths converted in large numbers to Islam as did some Jews and a great number of Christians; and Gothic identity has left a faint echo in the Arabic name *al-quti*—the Goth. The mental map of Christianity was shifting. Even though the Pyrenees were for centuries a *marca*—a border territory, march—with intermittent violent encounters, al-Andalus—Muslim Spain—exerted vast cultural influence upon the rest of Europe.

The shape of Europe was thus dramatically affected by these conquests. They created in Iberia and southwest Gaul a culture so diverse and alliances so unexpected, as to challenge our concept of medieval Europe. Iberia also saw the coexistence of Jews, Muslims, and Christians—as unequal neighbours—in a manner which has

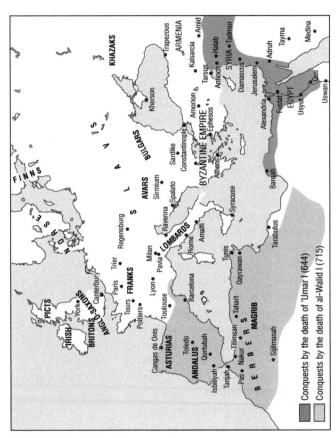

Map 2. Islam in Europe and the Mediterranean c.750

Conquests by the death of 'Umar I (644)

Conquests by the death of al-Walid I (715)

come to be known as *convivencia*—living together—within a sphere of Arabic culture. We will return to this legacy for Europe in a later chapter. Another important concept—crusade—was born in these parts. By the 11th century knights from Francia—as Frankish Gaul came to be known—received papal blessing when they joined the efforts to conquer lands ruled by Muslims, and thus to join what came to be known as the *reconquista*.

The balance of political power in Christian Europe now shifted northwards, away from the dangerous Mediterranean. There, the Merovingian Franks gained prominence through conquest and consolidation of their administration of vast lands, which reached from Denmark to Saxony to Lombardy.

Court ritual and art emulated the sole source of imperial majesty—the imperial court in Constantinople. But as the Frankish kingdom prospered, a rivalry developed between the two polities. In a period of particular turmoil in the Byzantine Empire, theologians and courtiers in the Frankish court even challenged the Empire's leadership in religious matters. During the rule of Empress Irene (752–803)—and exploiting the political vulnerability which often accompanied the rise of a woman to the throne—they penned the *Libri Carolini* in 794. This tract discussed and extolled the role of images in Christian worship, a polemic against the iconoclastic austerities which had recently been adopted by three successive Byzantine emperors. Political hegemony received religious endorsement in Rome on Christmas day 800, when Charles the Great (*c.*742–814), king of the Franks—also known as Charlemagne—had himself crowned by the pope as emperor.

Beyond the old Roman provinces the Roman legacy was developing into something new. While Roman cities and law were densely available in Italy, Gaul, and Spain, they were less visible and accessible in northern Europe. Yet *Romanitas* in the 7th or 8th century was invested in other ideas and practices.

2. The chapel of Charlemagne's palace in Aachen, built between 792 and 805. The debt to Roman architecture is evident in barrel-shaped vaults, the cupola crowning the chapel, and marble columns brought from Italy

The language of religion, ritual, and learning was Latin, and churchmen were best placed to teach its uses. Classical learning was favoured because it was extremely useful for communication and governance. So, for example, the *Rhetorica ad Herennium* (*Rhetoric for Herennius*), a textbook on rhetoric composed in the

90s BCE, remained one of the most widely used manuals for any holder of public office in church or state. Every monastery had a copy, every cathedral, and every court. Similarly, the book of medical recipes, *Materials of Medicine*, by Dioscorides (*c.*40–90 CE), an army surgeon from Asia Minor, was one of the most popular books well into the 16th century. It was cherished for its diagnostic insights and for the botanical cures it offered. A lively engagement with the classical tradition characterized many areas of life in these centuries. Books written in antiquity were copied, but also annotated; medieval users added glosses and even practical illustrations to books of medicine and geography, history, and poetry. These traditions were appreciated for their benefits, tested against contemporary needs.

Charlemagne explored the possibilities of Christian culture and Roman education in his court at Aachen (Figure 2). He assembled a formidable group of scholars and administrators, who made tangible the idea of Christian–Roman–European rule. Emperors were greater than kings; they led Christian life and extended it to new peoples; they legislated and determined in issues of faith. Emperors had at their disposal not only unique *regalia*—crowns, rings, and sceptres—but incomes, rights, and rituals of court. In the 10th century a Saxon dynasty—the Ottonians—established itself as heir to the Holy Roman Empire between 936 and 1024. The Ottonians reinforced their claims to ascendancy by arranging marriages with the Byzantine imperial family, and by promoting—as Charlemagne had done—enterprises of conquest, court art and architecture. Fittingly, they were also great patrons of monasteries and their learning.

The Byzantine Empire was experiencing vast change, as its territories were depleted by Muslim extension into Syria, north Africa, southern Italy, and Sicily. But an arena for expansion existed to its north and northwest, among the Bulgars, Poles, and the people of Rus'. Christianity was brought by Greek missionaries like the saintly brothers, Cyril and Methodius, to

Moravia and Pannonia. Byzantine culture spread through church rites, conveyed in the new alphabet which the missionaries helped to devise, and which developed into the Cyrillic alphabet, still used today throughout eastern Europe and parts of Asia. The Byzantine Empire was battered by the movement of peoples like the Seljuks from central Asia in the 10th and 11th centuries. The nomadic Seljuks converted to Islam and became a dynamic military force in pursuit of conquest for their new faith. The waning of Byzantine religious solidarity and influence in the West was marked from 1054 by the schism between Greek and Latin bishops over the theology of the Trinity. The history of the Byzantine Empire will be told in the *Very Short Introduction* to Byzantium.

For all the challenges it faced, the Byzantine Empire could still be an important ally in European enterprises. When an armed pilgrimage—later to be styled 'crusade'—left Europe in 1096 with the aim of offering help to the Christians of the east and regaining access for Christians to the Holy Land, its leaders expected that help would be forthcoming—in food, troops, and logistics—from the Byzantine Empire. Emperor Alexios I Comnenos (1056–1118) was, in fact, alarmed by this assumption. His daughter and biographer, Anna Comnena (1083–1153), describes with bemusement the arrival of the contingents from the West, each expecting to be received in style and supported.

Even further north

While this transformation of the Mediterranean and Gaul was under way, change also characterized the British Isles, Scandinavia, and central Europe. Following the withdrawal of Roman forces around 400, throughout the 5th century Angles, Saxons, Frisians, and some Franks migrated and settled in southern and eastern England, often penetrating further inland though the rivers Ouse, Trent, and Nene. The Germanic settlers sought agricultural land, and often displaced native Celtic communities, forced to move further west and north. This period was to be remembered and re-created in later centuries in the traditions associated with Arthur, king of the Britons, who was revived in the 12th century, and would remain thereafter the epitome of a chivalrous Christian king.

Southern England became a region of active mission *c*.600 with the arrival of the delegation sent by Pope Gregory I. Like elsewhere in Europe, conversion was led by rulers, animated by charismatic missionaries, and often bolstered by Christian queens. Throughout the British Isles the influences of holy men from Ireland was felt. The Life of St Columba (d. 597), written a century after his death by the monk Adomnán, describes the holy man at work from the island of Iona off the west coast of Scotland, admonishing chieftains, prophesying the results of battles, exorcising demons, and confronting magicians with his own cures. Irish influence affected the style of religious life—the calendar, the monastic ethos—often at odds with Roman–Continental practices. From Christian Francia abbess Bertila (d. *c*.704) sent books and relics to these 'new' Christians. In time the term 'Christendom' was coined by an English writer, and figures from the British Isles became iconic Christian leaders: the Northumbrian monk-historian, Bede (673–735), whose history of the church was highly appreciated throughout Europe; or Alcuin of York (*c*.735–804), who spent much of his life in Charlemagne's court, leading reform of education and acting as diplomat between England and the Continent.

This integrated northern European world, Christian and increasingly organized around dynastic rule, was about to be devastated by violent disruption: raids by Norsemen, first attested in 789. Several decades of violent contact followed, first of the more exposed outposts, like the monastic islands of Lindisfarne or Iona. The north of England, east Midlands, and parts of East Anglia, as well as northern parts of Francia, were all affected. By the mid-9th century a period of settlement and consolidation was under way,

3. The Hiddensee Treasure comprises 16 items of purest gold: brooch, necklace, and pendants probably made for the Danish king, Harald Bluetooth (*c.*935–*c.*986). The Norsemen—Vikings—traded from Dublin to Rus' and hoarded their wealth in luxury goods

and York and Dublin became important Norse trading centres. Ultimately, after decades of dislocation, enduring forms of cohabitation emerged: the Norse leader, Rollo, paid homage to the king of France in 911, for the terrain of Normandy. In Wessex, the Viking challenge had prompted the enhancement of administration and defence under King Alfred (849–99) (Figure 3).

Christian ideas and practices were now disseminated to those who joined the European commonwealth as a package of religious teaching, liturgy, law, and letters. These processes were mutual and reciprocal. Magyars, Bohemians, and Norse people continued to live in kinship groups with their intricate patterns of mutual protection, immersed in a heroic ethos. They were choosing to join the Christian world with its big idea: salvation offered by a suffering God. For them the figure of Christ was that of a hero, who had triumphed over death.

Europe c.1000

By the year 1000 the European population had begun to grow, and for some 300 years food production grew too, more than matching the demand. This meant that some people from every rural community could move to towns and cities and develop specialized skills, safe in the knowledge that food would be available there for purchase. Urban growth occurred both in existing urban centres—old Roman cities—and in thousands of new towns. This process has left its mark on European place-names which announced their newness: *Neu*ville, *Neu*stadt, *New*town, Castel*nuovo*, or *Neu*kirchen. Cities became hubs of cultural activity—in cathedrals, schools, and town halls—alongside the traditional rural cultural strongholds: monasteries and aristocratic households.

Resources, enthusiasm, and talent were now invested in new institutions of religion and learning, and that is why a century ago the American historian Charles Homer Haskins (1870–1937) called the period 'The Renaissance of the Twelfth Century'. Members of the social elite, enriched by the agricultural boom, founded monasteries where their families, past, present, and future, would be commemorated in prayer; townspeople supported schools for training in scribal arts, law, and medicine. Conquests led to waves of building, like that following the Norman Conquest in England, or when territories were conquered for Christian rule in Iberia. Dynasts marked their unique destinies in prestige projects like the abbey of St Denis north of Paris for the Capetian dynasty, or the rebuilding of the church of the Holy Sepulchre in the crusader-founded Kingdom of Jerusalem.

While much classical learning was well established in Europe, some classical lore became available to Europeans only in the 12th and 13th centuries through a two-step process of transmission. In the 7th and 8th centuries Greek learning was translated into Arabic following the Muslim conquests and the establishment of a court in Baghdad. After 1100 a great deal of translation took place from Arabic into Latin, led by scholars from Muslim Spain—al-Andalus—like Peter Alfonsi (c.1062–1110). Peter was born a Jew and converted to Christianity in 1106. He translated from Arabic and Persian moral and ethical tales, wrote on astronomy, and composed polemical works against Judaism. He moved between the spheres of learning in Hebrew, Arabic, and Latin. Peter travelled widely—he may have practised as court physician to Henry I (1068–1135)—and his books were copied and enthusiastically received.

The 12th and 13th centuries saw a remarkable consolidation of political units and increased European integration. As we shall see in some detail in the chapters below, population growth went hand in hand with the development of cities, diversification of trade, and expansion in the territories of Christian Europe. An elite educated in Latin served kings and popes, bishops and princes; a system of parishes brought all Europeans into the reach of ecclesiastical instruction, ritual, and discipline. Some parts of Europe became perennial war zones: the Scottish borders, the shifting Christian/Muslim frontiers in Iberia and the Near East, and the Baltic region where crusades against pagans were waged.

Violence within polities was increasingly tracked down and contained by royal administrations of justice, supported by local magistrates and with the participation of local communities.

All this was underpinned by law-codes and customs, newly codified and disseminated. In the 1140s authoritative texts of church law were assembled into the *Decretum*, a concordance of the Christian legal tradition which aimed to harmonize apparent contradictions. It was followed in each century by new collections and commentaries, a shared legal heritage for European church courts. Kingdoms produced their own codes, but also allowed other spheres of jurisdiction, like those of landlords on their manors, and town councils over their markets and citizens. Legal expertise developed in hubs of commercial activity, like the Italian cities, and some groups regulated their own affairs, like Jews and Muslims in Spain, and foreign merchants in Venice.

Dynastic ambitions caused monarchs to build effective bureaucracies for the management of their finances in peace and war, and for the delivery of justice. Occasionally resources had to be mustered in desperate attempts to defend territories, as the rulers of Poland, Hungary, and Rus' did in the early 1240s against Mongol attacks. But dynastic ambitions also led to expensive wars of conquest, like Charles of Anjou's seizure of Sicily in the 1260s, Edward I's conquest and settlement of Wales two decades later, or the Hundred Years War (1334–1453) between England and France. The later 13th century also saw a decline in the rate of growth and ultimately the marks of famine and economic vulnerability in many regions: the price of foodstuffs rose, and the size of peasants' land-holdings shrank under population pressure. In some regions cash crops had displaced food crops—dyestuffs were planted aplenty in Picardy and vines in Gascony—so the balance of humans, animals, and food became increasingly precarious. Around 1300 the Little Ice Age set in, and its wet and cold meant that the extent of European land suitable for cultivation decreased considerably (Map 3).

The famine which ravaged northwest Europe (1314–17), and the great calamity of the Black Death (1347–52) put all the

Map 3. Europe and its neighbours c.1300

arrangements we have been surveying to a deadly test. Unprecedented flooding and fiercely cold winters from autumn 1314 meant that agricultural yields were down—sometimes by 40 per cent. However integrated the European economy had become, it failed to provide food where it was needed. This failure was exacerbated by the tendency of landlords to hoard foodstuffs and thus speculate. Just as the next generations were beginning to recover and population to grow again, the Black Death—what is now commonly agreed to have been the bubonic plague—reached Europe. The disease had spread across central Asia over the preceding decades, reaching Europe by vessels that traded between the Black Sea and Italy in 1347. This disease was initially borne by fleas that had fed on infected rats and then passed the disease on to humans. Infected humans developed pustules on their bodies, especially around the lymph nodes, and a high fever; they usually died within ten days. A pneumonic version had a swifter effect, with death coming even more quickly. While mortality rates differed across European regions and settlements, it is estimated that close to half of the population perished. Nor did it stop there, as the plague returned in the 1360s and 1370s, and in many areas in the 15th century too.

The world was truly turned upside down as disease, loss, and bereavement affected all Europeans. The population did not reach early-14th century levels again until well into the 16th. So many of the assumptions about the European economy had to be rethought. Labour was in great demand, but less food was required to feed the depleted population. Rulers attempted to intervene and direct the response by legislating the changes away with fixed wages and restricted worker mobility. It is not surprising, therefore, that the later 14th and 15th centuries saw a great deal of urban and rural unrest all over Europe. Landlords sought to move from the labour-intensive cultivation of arable lands, to more diverse activities such as mining, pasture, and fisheries. Cities became more aware of the responsibilities they had in maintaining public health through care for urban spaces.

Europeans invented new ways of commemorating their many dead; they also became more impatient with those deemed to be lazy, and without settled abode or regular employment, the 'undeserving' poor.

Europe continued to change in shape and population size in the later centuries of our period. The Baltic region became part of Europe following the conquest of Livonia by the Teutonic Order in the 13th century and its settlement by German-speaking colonists; the Greek-speaking Byzantine Empire was conquered by the Ottomans in 1453; and Christian rulers conquered large parts of al-Andalus, a process which ended with the fall of Granada in 1492. Europeans of many ethnicities and religious affiliations confronted the Mongols in Hungary, Austria, and Poland. Crusaders continued to imagine the conquest of north Africa and the reconquest of the Holy Land; one group came upon the Canary Islands in the late 14th century and established vestigial rule there, with papal blessing. Throughout these later centuries Europeans lived abroad in enclaves and trading stations—*funduq*s—in Alexandria, Damascus, Constantinople, Karakorum, and Jerusalem. Along the trade routes pilgrims travelled too, as did curious scholars and would-be missionaries. By the end of our period the eastern Mediterranean was ruled by the Ottoman dynasty, and to the west explorations of the coast of Africa were encouraged and financed by the kings of Portugal. It is common to end this period in 1492 with Columbus' journey which saw his arrival in the 'Indies'. Yet Columbus seems far more to belong to the traditions of European travel, cartography, and royal patronage of trade, infused with a sense of Christian mission.

The 'Middle' Ages? What remains of this concept of 'middleness'? Not much.

Chapter 2
People and their life-styles

It is often assumed that people of this period were vastly different from us. This is not a helpful assumption. Then, as now, individuals aimed to live the best lives possible while struggling to make ends meet, fulfilling the expectations of institutions, and trying to satisfy some of their desires. Endowing people in the past with a sphere of autonomy, and even of choice—however modest—is sometimes described by historians as considering their *agency*. Thinking about agency does not mean ignoring the many factors over which people had no or little control, like the brutal realities of hunger, disease, and violence. We should think of people in the past as possessing self-awareness and the capacity to experience subtle feelings and complex thoughts. Some scholars have identified the 'discovery of the individual' in the 12th, or the birth of affective relations in the family in the 18th century. Yet, as we shall see, our sources—ranging from wills to poetry, from visual imagery to testimonies in courts of law—show individuals from across the social spectrum displaying emotions familiar to us: loyalty, jealousy, greed, hope, and passionate love.

This chapter will explore the routines of family and community life in rural settlements and urban centres, in private and in public. Some activities were associated with kinship, others with the search for protection. People sometimes joined others in their efforts—in a trade guild or a religious fraternity—but they also sought out patronage and guidance from individuals who were stronger, richer, or more expert than themselves.

Free, unfree, or only partly free

The capacity to act in the world was affected by an individual's legal status: free, slave, or serf. Roman law recognized the conditions of freedom and slavery, and slavery remained a European institution throughout our period, though with great variation. The law of the church decreed that Christians could not be enslaved, yet some did indeed live as slaves. Indigenous slavery on large Roman estates persisted at the beginning of our period, and existed alongside the constant stream of slaves taken in battles on Europe's eastern borderlands. The word *slav* became synonymous with the word 'slave' (*sclavus* in Latin). The survey of estates conducted by Abbot Irminon of St Germain-des-Près outside Paris *c.*825 had 7,975 individuals living in 1,378 households, all bound to the estate. These were large households, with an average of 5.78 members. The Domesday Book, a vast survey of English lands, population, and resources, compiled in 1085–6 for William the Conqueror, shows how numerous slaves were on English estates, over 10 per cent of the population surveyed, though the status of slave soon disappears from our sources. Enslavement was used against Muslims and Jews in Catalonia and Aragon in punishment of a variety of political and sexual offences.

Dependent unfree men with skills could rise up the social scale through military and administrative service. In the Holy Roman Empire unfree *ministeriales* held land and married the daughters of noblemen; they commanded castles and in turn held courts of their own. The Hungarian *jobbágiones* were allowed freedom of movement and were mobilized in the 13th century in warfare against the Mongols, and in the 15th against the Turks. Another form of servile living was introduced to Europe in the late 14th century when black African slaves were sold for domestic service in Italian and Iberian cities. They were habitually released from slavery (manumitted) after a while, often remaining in domestic service, or working as artisans, musicians, or fishermen.

Those who were not slaves were not all free, for our period sees the development of a status of unfreedom which is not equal to slavery: it is serfdom. There were many routes to such servility: loss of an individual's land through poverty and debt, or through conquest followed by loss of land. The serf householder was attached to the land he and his family cultivated, and their tenure entailed important obligations which were the mark of servility. Serfs shared the produce of their labour with their lords, they were obliged to execute work at the lord's request, and they were limited in their right to travel. Serfs were often required to bring their corn for grinding in the lord's mill and their grapes to the lord's winepress, and to pay for a licence when they sought to marry outside the manor; a fine beast was paid to secure the passage of the serf's tenure to its heir. Their lives were hard, and often characterized by writers in our periods as being simple and rude. When bishop Rather of Verona around 930 wrote with guidance to Christians of all conditions, he advised the labourer: 'be not only fair, but hard-working, content with your lot, cheating no one, offending no one'.

Members of the serf's household were servile too. An Irish satirical poem of c.1060 expressed abuse of those at the bottom of the social scale, here associated with ploughing: 'o Domnall, dark and crooked, harsh and wrinkled... You grandson of a ploughman/[who is] filthy like a badger'. Serfs could be freed by manumission, either granted as a favour—as when a serf's son was freed in order to qualify for training to become a priest—or against payment. Even after manumission a vestige of unfreedom could linger, as in the case of those entitled *colliberti* on French estates. Serfs sometimes left their family holdings to join an army or to work in a town, and landlords' officials aimed to locate such fugitives and return them to the land. In periods of demographic growth, like the 12th and 13th centuries, servile folk were able to negotiate and pay manorial officials in order to move to a town. After the Black Death (1347–52) when demand for workers in cities was extremely high, young men and women departed from manors in great numbers, often leaving dependent old and young behind. The erosion of serfdom after 1350 meant that customs which burdened serfs were lightened, but so too were the obligations which secured the tenure of servile families.

Being a man and being a woman

Within these social worlds conventions related to being a man or a woman were highly consequential. Gendered attitudes sought to protect as well as control, to exalt as well as vilify women and femininity, while maleness served as an ideal, the state of humanity in the image of God. The details of this system differed by region, social sphere, and period, but everywhere gender was seen and asserted in rituals and public statements. Clothing, comportment, use of space, all served to display the gendered order of society. Frankish high-born nuns were buried in colourful clothes: Bathild (d. 680) in a red cloak with yellow fringes and Bertila (d. *c.*704) in a brown tunic with yellow trimming. Even in the harsh conditions of life in Greenland, items of clothing from *c.*1200 show that men wore garments dyed dark brown and black, women's dresses were decorated with patches of contrasting colours, and children were dressed in white and grey. Colour-coding is not a modern invention.

Most of the assumptions in secular and ecclesiastical law and much social custom agreed that women were weaker than men in their mental, moral, and physical capacities. The church taught that women and men could hope and strive for salvation, but also that women's nature tended towards sin. It followed that it was harder for women to deploy human reason—the gift of God—since they were distracted by their carnal nature, above all by their roaming wombs. This weakness of reason meant that they could not be placed in positions of authority over men, their superiors. Even the dedicated religious woman Ida of Barking was exhorted by the monk Osbert of Clare c.1136: 'Do not let lascivious mirth reduce you to your sex. Conquer the woman; conquer the flesh; conquer desire'.

Such ideas were embedded in the system of ethics and science inherited from antiquity according to which the human person resided in a body which was also home to the soul. The person emerged from the combination of matter and spirit, and each individual was a unique blend of humours, each with its particular qualities: choleric—mostly hot; sanguine—mostly moist; phlegmatic—mostly cold; or melancholic—mostly dry. The grid of natural bodily conditions was understood to be in flux, and the balance at any moment was affected by planetary movements, but also by the routines of eating and bodily care undertaken by individuals. Men were vigorous in their heat, so religious men sought to lessen their distracting masculinity and sexual drive by eating cooling foods, like vegetables, and by avoiding spices. Colder men grew a thinner beard and had smaller testicles; they were more like women. Women, in turn, who sought to become more 'virile' and give up their femininity might seek sources of heat to compensate for their natural wet and cold complexions. The spiritual guide to the religious woman Catherine of Siena (1347–80) described her seeking out, in the public baths, the hottest and most sulphurous streams of water.

Family and marriage

Most people spent work and leisure within the family sphere. In both towns and villages the family was a unit of work. On the peasant holding or in the artisan's workshop, men, women, and children worked together. Households included not only close family members, but also dependants such as needy relatives, servants, apprentices, and even the poor. The household was ordered under the rule of a male head, and in his absence, sometimes, that of his wife.

Marriage was the most pervasive, yet contested, social institution. Roman law defined marriage as a contract, while Germanic custom endowed marriage with the quality of a family enterprise, an alliance between families through their young; alongside marriage it recognized other less binding alliances. To these traditions was added Christian sexual morality, which sought to make marriage a framework for virtuous Christian lives. Discussion began in earnest as Christian thinkers—like Augustine, bishop of Hippo in North Africa (354–430)—grappled with the reality of mass Christianity. His approach was above all theological, an exploration of marriage as a remedy against sin. He opened the way to an understanding of Christian marriage, though some thinkers continued to insist that married life was inferior to the life of heroic chastity.

The conventions and exigencies which operated on men and women were complex and varied. Underlying this variety was an understanding of identity rooted in sexual difference. It directed men to assume responsibility and care for wives, daughters, and sisters, and it also allowed them to control women's property, and direct their lives. Men habitually used violence in asserting authority, even as they expressed deep grief at the loss of a partner. The Carolingian scholar and courtier Einhard spoke of missing his wife Imma (d. 835) 'every day, in every action, in every undertaking'. He was consoled in turn by letters from his friend Lupus of Ferrières, praising her since 'although a mere woman in body, she had achieved in spirit the stature of man'. Richard II (1367–1400), king of England, famously mourned the loss of his wife, for the rest of his life, and even after he remarried.

The Christian idea of marriage as sacramental, monogamous, oriented towards procreation, and for life, was fully codified in the 12th century. Disseminated vigorously through canon law, Christian marriage seemed like an intrusive innovation, and centuries passed before it was accepted by Europeans. This view of marriage was propagated by the Church, led by activist popes—many of whom were trained in the law. It sought to bring the most intimate and consequential aspects of life—family, progeny, inheritance, sexuality—within a Christian ethical and legal sphere. It did so by considering marriage a personal moral act, by making laws to match, and by providing religious instruction to inform laity and clergy alike. As marriage became a sacrament any infringement related to it was claimed as the business of church courts and was regulated by priests and bishops.

Sacramental marriage was an irreversible ritual, a transfer of grace to two freely consenting partners. Experts in church law—canon lawyers—explored all possibilities: What was the minimal age of marriage? How binding was the expression of mere intent to marry? Could Christian marriage be overruled by dissenting relatives? Could a married person leave to pursue the greater virtue of monastic life? And what if a marriage was never consummated sexually? Such questions became the stuff of legal discussion and life dramas; in church courts witnesses described disappointments and sorrows in minute detail. These courts accepted the testimony of women, so they recorded them speaking of heartbreak, broken promises, sexual humiliation, and more.

The church aimed to promote partnerships in conformity with biblical definitions of incest. Religious advisors sought to move rulers towards a Christian sexual morality, but they also understood the limitations to such attempts. Pope Gregory I allowed the missionary to southern England, Augustine of Canterbury (d. 604), to act with leniency with the recently converted English on the issue of licit marriage partners. Charlemagne, avid promoter of Christian learning, had many wives and complex webs of paternity. He was also described as having an incestuous relationship with his sister Gisla (757–810), who later became the abbess of Chelles. The scope of incest waxed and waned. At baptism new spiritual kin were created—godfather and godmother—so they and theirs entered the circles of kin forbidden in marriage. By the 12th century church law allowed marriage only to those separated by seven degrees of kinship. Such strictures were hard to live by. By 1215 the church had relaxed the degrees of prohibited kinship, to four; even that was a rule hard to enforce within small rural communities or within the elite marriage circle open to royals. Ideas about incest remained a subject of fascination. Manuals for confessors instructed priests to probe their parishioners about it with direct questions, and preaching addressed the topic too. Literary works also explored incest, like the German verse poem *Gregorius* of *c.*1200, by Hartmann von Aue (*c.*1165–*c.*1215), about a saint who was the product of incestuous union.

By the 13th century Christian marriage was taught widely, and so became over the centuries a recognized pathway. To traditional rituals of betrothal and marriage—celebrated by families and within communities—were now added church rituals. There was often the blessing at the church door; and when children came along, there was baptism to bind family and church even closer, and churching of mothers—a form of purification and reintegration of them into the community—after the ordeal—and pollution—of childbirth. For all its uniqueness, in sermons the life of Mary and Joseph was upheld as an ideal.

Christian marriage promoted ideals of conjugality and complementarity. Men and women were different, but could help each other in making a Christian life. The conjugal debt was conceived as a mutual duty to have sex in marriage. It was taught in sermons as an obligation on women to overcome qualms about sexual contact—due to illness, personal aversion, the restrictions of Lent, or menstruation—and respond to their husband's desire. In the 15th century an influential voice opposed the tyranny of the 'debt'. The Tuscan Franciscan preacher Bernardino of Siena (1380–1444), wise to women's dilemmas from hearing their confessions, taught the husband's right to instruct and correct, and the wife's duty to obey, respect, and exhort. But he also decried coercive sex as an infringement on the duty of affection. Bernardino's sermons restated the tenor of Augustine's words a thousand years earlier, with a Tuscan twist: marriage was for the bridling of desire, and should not be delayed, lest men become used to having sex with each other, a 'pestiferous' habit which is hard to break.

Parents and priests encouraged young adults to settle in family units. Whatever their youthful sexual experiences, and these were often within same-sex environments of training and work, most people married. Many even remarried, and in this way produced multigenerational families and complex webs of inheritance and sentiment. Towards the end of our period, religious image and narrative caught up with this social reality. The Holy Family—Mary, Joseph, and the child Christ—was represented within a rich web of relations, in which Anne—Mary's mother—doted over her many grandchildren, the product of her three consecutive marriages. Parish churches in Germany displayed the family arranged as a sculpted group: the two holy women and the child Christ to the fore, and Anne's other daughters with their children—Christ's cousins—around them; at the back were four men: Joseph and Anne's three husbands (Figure 4). Men and women, young and old saw their own family relationships mirrored in such images.

If sex in marriage was oriented towards producing sons and daughters, then any impediment to intercourse provided a cause for annulment; and if marriage was a sacrament freely entered, any suggestion of coercion could similarly make void the resulting 'forced'

4. A painted sculpture, of c.1485, from a German parish portraying a family with women and children to the fore: the Holy Kinship of the child Christ

marriage. Anxiety about the ability to establish a family is palpable in many different types of sources. People resorted to magic, medicine, prayer, and pilgrimage in the hope of being able to have children.

Households

With marriage a household was created, and most Europeans formed new homes after marriage. These were units of work: on the family's agricultural land or in a workshop. Knightly and aristocratic families ran estates as household enterprises from a castle, a fortified manor house, or—as was the case with some Italian families—an urban palace. Women, apprentices, grooms, and servants helped run these households, which were represented by the male head of household in law, finance, politics, and civic ritual.

Royal and aristocratic courts were at once the home to an extended family, a household, as well as the headquarters of a bureaucratic and political enterprise. In the earlier centuries royal courts were almost always on the move. The Merovingian kings of the Franks travelled between their estates with their court about them, supported by the produce and labour of their lands and serfs, as well as by the hospitality which religious houses were obliged to offer to their benefactors. One such courtier—the holder of the all-important role of *maior domus*, chief steward to the household—Charles Martel (*c.*688–741), assumed so much power and influence that his sons—Peppin and Carloman—became kings of the Frankish lands after his death. Peppin's son, Charlemagne, created a capital, the very grandest kind of household, at Aachen. The group of priests and servants which surrounded a bishop and animated his cathedral came to be known as *familia*—a family household of sorts—and provided its celibate members with the support and care that biological families were usually expected to offer.

Women's work was central to any household's wellbeing and it took place in all spheres. The *Life of St Gerard*, the martyred bishop known in Hungarian as Gellért (980–1046), describes the bishop on his travels hearing the sounds of millstones accompanied by a woman's voice. His travelling companion explained that she was grinding corn, rotating the mill, yet singing 'in a sweet and merry manner'. Coroners' records from 13th century England show that women suffered accidents in the course of agricultural labour: in fields, barns, and when using heavy and sharp metal implements.

Women's work involved skill and coordination at home, in workshops, and in fields, and they were trained informally by other women. Everywhere women gathered and prepared food, tended to domestic animals, and made textiles. A wall-painting from the Danish church of Kirkerup, near Roskilde (c.1330) shows a woman spinning yarn while balancing two swaddled children on her hips (Figure 5). Spinning, weaving, and sewing garments required the use of specialized tools. Finds from 13th century Greenland include needles, scissors, seam smoothers, and weights for looms. A great deal of specialized knowledge went into assembling of wools and animal hair which were made into yarn, and coloured with natural dyes made of lichen, woad, and even tinted brown by dipping in iron-rich water.

In cities women participated in family artisan workshops, often working 'front of shop', selling the finished goods from shops on

5. A wall painting from the Danish church of Kirkerup of c.1330 depicting a mother with two swaddled babies tied to her body, busy at her spinning. Situated near the Expulsion from Eden, it links toil to Eve's sin

the ground floor. In the households of notaries, doctors, and merchants daughters learned to read, write, and compute, a useful preparation for adult life within such a household of their own. Women sold homemade goods, and often worked with the byproducts of the family business, like turning tallow into candles. In the later part of our period women worked in textile manufacture from home, often in groups, and also provided a growing workforce of domestic servants, much in demand after the Black Death. Women hawked cheap goods and sold pre-cooked food, since maintaining a private kitchen was the privilege of better-off townspeople. The local legal framework determines how we get to know such women: a brewer of Ingatestone in Essex accused in 1344 of serving unfit ale was represented in court by her husband, who also paid the fine; but in Marseille, the Jewish midwife Floreta d'Ays faced in 1403 a malpractice suit on her own.

Historians used to think that emotional cherishing of children was the invention of the Enlightenment. This is quite wrong. The household was the focus of nurture and care for the young. From the peasantry to aristocratic elites, all social groups developed ways of training the young for healthy and productive lives. Even modest families travelled to shrines, seeking cure for their children. Frankish grave-goods buried with children include child-size weapons and toys. Complex webs of coercion and encouragement governed attitudes to the young within these patriarchal communities, and so privileged in many instances the old over the young, sons over daughters, and close kin over lesser relations. Women were expected to train children, and as norms of Christian behaviour spread and became better established in Europe, so did the role of mothers and female kin as first educators. The Psalms, the Creed, the widely used prayers *Ave Maria* and *Pater Noster*, and edifying religious tales were taught in households in the mother tongue and were integrated into family life.

Tough decisions had to be taken in order to secure the future of the young. By the 10th century most landholding families in large parts of Europe—England, France, and parts of the Empire—recognized the land inherited by the father as patrimony, to be passed on to the heir. The patrimony gave the family its name—this period sees the fixing of such surnames, *cognomina*—like *de Coucy* or *de Bouillon*. Younger sons were apportioned lands perhaps more recently acquired, less central to the family's prestige. In an extreme case in point, William the Conqueror's eldest, Robert Curthose, inherited Normandy in 1087—the family patrimony—and his younger brother, the future Henry I, inherited that more recent acquisition—the kingdom of England.

The ideal heir to a family's name and lands was an adult male, but often this was simply not possible. In these situations women were made rulers of men and held important positions of power. As he prepared for succession, Henry I of England had only an illegitimate son and so he made efforts to secure the inheritance for his daughter Matilda (1102–67). He bound the magnates of the kingdom by oaths to accept her as heir, and thus to secure dynastic and political continuity. Yet, when the time came, this did not work. The English aristocracy preferred a man of lesser birth, who was well-known, -liked, and -tried in battle: Stephen of Blois. England was soon plunged into years of strife. In the 13th century, the counts of Flanders, some of Europe's greatest dynasts, made their daughters heirs with greater success. Within cities, the statutes of guilds that regulated household workshops allowed guild widows to run workshops until their son/heir reached majority.

Primogeniture—inheritance by the eldest son—came to prevail not only among landed people, but also in more modest households: the inheritance of servile land or of craft workshops in towns throughout Europe. Some regions maintained partible inheritance—parts of Kent, still in the 13th century, Wales, southern France—and confronted the challenges it posed:

provision for several heirs always meant that a viable land holding could be reduced within a generation or two to fragments that barely supported any of its holders. Most families combined several strategies for the sake of the young: advantageous marriage, training in a craft, migration, land-clearance, and the acquisition of a new tenancy, professional formation in preparation for careers in law, as clergy, or as bureaucratic servants in great households, cities, or royal courts. As to daughters, they were apportioned a dowry with the aim of attracting a good match, the dowry being a way of sharing the family's wealth.

Rural settlements

Most people lived in rural settlements and in many forms. There were the densely settled nucleated villages as in southern England, northern France, and Pomerania, where arable farming meant that villagers lived surrounded by the fields they tilled. At the centre of some villages was a green or a square, a public space around a well, and sometimes near the local church. Fishing villages along European coasts shared some distinctive features. Be they in Norway, Ireland, or Sicily, they were often surrounded by sea-marshes and salt-pans; the sex ratio of their population was often skewed, with a super-abundance of women. Some villages were surrounded by protective walls, others encompassed hamlets—neighbouring clusters of farms—spread out and isolated. The layout of rural settlements reflected the landscape, work and livelihood of their inhabitants, as well as the circumstances of original implantation.

It is commonly thought that rural settlements were unchanging features of history, but the reality is more complex and interesting. While some settlements in southern Europe were indeed very old, migration, raiding, transhumance, and conquest all contributed to change in village life. Think of the wooden fabric of the most modest northern European habitation: those who lived in them in the 6th and 7th centuries periodically upped sticks—literally—with their livestock, and abandoned rotting wooden structures to set up elsewhere. Movement characterized the lives of villagers in the Alpine region, where part of the population spent several months a year away from the village, seeking pasture and some protection from severe weather conditions. Hundreds of villages in Castile, from the 13th century, saw seasonal movement of vast numbers of sheep to pasture and back. Transhumance transformed the shape of these communities for months at a time: the movement of some three million sheep from north to south removed men and beasts alike. At the same time, and in consequence, towns and cities along their pathways—the *cañadas*—saw their population swell.

Rural settlements often centred around a *villa* held by a churchman or a notable. In Iberia Roman villas endured as economic units and family homes even under Muslim rulers. While grain production was at the core, there was pig and sheep rearing, and crafts in locally grown raw materials like wool and linen. Such settlements formed the core of fortified seats of lordship by the year 1000, made strong by the local lord—*seigneur*. Castles were built to secure safety and in display of authority. Fortified communities marked the landscape as a refuge in time of war for those who inhabited neighbouring lands. Monteriggioni, north of Siena, was situated for decades at the border between the territories of Florence and Siena; it was surrounded by a 'crown' of towers—14 of which still survive—and offered refuge to peasants in the surrounding lowlands whenever those two cities clashed.

By the year 1000, relations between lords and their vassals, manorial landlords and their serfs, offered the basis for political and military organization and for economic development. Relations of lordship and tenure framed the lives of most Europeans, the most powerful and the least. On the basis of these dispositions of landed wealth and natural resources, a whole array of cultural and personal values developed: loyalty, chivalry, justice, liberality, communal responsibility, and more.

In large parts of Europe rural settlements existed within a system of land tenure that has been named since the 17th century as 'feudal'. This term is often used to characterize the arrangements whereby land was held by men in a hierarchical and nested system: each vassal held land from a lord and in return offered that lord loyalty and advice. Lord and vassal were bound through a ceremony at which the latter offered homage, sealed with a kiss. The land held within this relationship could include a combination of one or more estates; in the highest echelons it amounted to a county, duchy, or even a kingdom—their population, resources, and related jurisdiction. Versions are to be found from the Hebrides to Hungary, from Tuscany to Norway, but its history and manifestations are highly diverse, far more than a sole '-ism' can convey. That is why historians now qualify their use of the term 'feudalism' or avoid it altogether.

The historian Marc Bloch (1886–1944) once remarked that every parcel of land could be called 'mine' by several persons: those who worked it, those who held the estate from a higher lord, the higher lord, and the king who granted it to that higher lord. Some lands were never turned into fiefs, but were worked under the supervision of the lord's official, a bailiff who supervised the hired labour as well as the work of serfs. These bailiffs—*sirvents*, or *sergents*—ran the estates, interacted with the rural workers in the local idiom, and summoned them to the manor court for infringements; they were never popular members of the rural community.

Serfs were obliged to share not only the crops they grew and the animals they tended, but also their labour, by providing work days to their lord. This was usually exacted in the form of agricultural labour, at sowing or harvest, just when their own holding required urgent attention. Whenever we look at a castle or at earthworks and wonder how they were built with the technology available a thousand years ago, we must remember that lords had access to a great deal of cheap labour from the landless, and to free labour from their serfs. Such labour services could also be exacted as cartage, hewing of stone, mining, and more.

Political change affected the rhythms of life in rural communities. After the Norman Conquest of England castles were built everywhere, at the centre of cities where they displaced tens of habitations at a time, and in strategically important regions, like the Welsh Marches, first in wood and later in stone. As one views these impressive structures it is clear that effective organization of labour and resources went into their making. Lords in charge of vast estates and dependent serfs could raise the required labour, command the required timber for construction, and could allocate portions of income from their estates towards the building. This was the very terrain where Offa, King of Mercia (r. 757–96), had built a dyke supported by earthworks, 300 years earlier. The archaeological remains from fishing villages of the Hebrides reflect the effect of conquest on economic life: before the advent of Norwegian influence and ultimately hegemony in the 10th century, the finds contained a wide range of fish bones—both in middens and in processing deposits; later on there is a clear concentration on cod and hake. The islanders' fishing habits were influenced by their incorporation into the Norwegian sphere of dominion, whose fish yields made them leaders in the European trade in dried fish. The introduction of grain-drying technology to the Hebrides in the form of kilns is evident in this period, as is that of black oat and rye, both part of a general move towards more intensive arable farming. This economic incorporation may also explain the new prominence of flax—introduced from Norway—whose oil was so useful in the treatment of wood and essential for boat-making.

Religious houses were usually granted estates at their foundation, and received more from benefactors over the centuries in return for prayer. They acted as a collective 'lord', and managed lands, often very effectively. Able to accumulate over centuries, untouched by sibling strife and the need to apportion dowries, religious houses amassed considerable wealth and so invested in substantial projects: bridge-building, drying of marshes, woodland clearance, and the construction of stylish buildings. Religious houses literally towered over the countryside, their church often the product of decades of labour by country people—in quarrying stone, preparing timber, construction, and carting.

Food security was affected in every region by a variety of interlocking causes such as weather, safety, and disease. We gain glimpses of the challenges of hunger, from the provisions made by landlords—of grain for food and for sowing—at time of need, as recorded in their accounts. And dearth produced fantasies of plenty, like the Land of Cokaigne, occasionally imagined in poems: a land where it rained meatballs and pancakes, where roasted chickens flew straight into the mouths of the hungry. Local rituals and expert magic were also deployed—despite official disapproval—to avert storms or make life-giving rains fall.

The rural settlement—the village—was the site of important solidarities within families and between neighbours. In the course of the Christianization of Europe, most villages became ecclesiastical units too. The village produced food, and yielded tithes—a tenth of the produce or earnings to the church; the village was home to families whose young required baptism and its dead burial. At the same time, those who owned estates and governed lives—knightly and noble landlords—were increasingly drawn into a close relationship with the church, its laws and its norms, and sought to spread these on their estates. Where neighbours were so co-dependent, reputation was all-important. Rural communities took slander seriously, as an Irish phrase put it, 'No wise…man should doubt that blood is shed by words', and slander became a sin punished by canon law, as an act against charity.

The wave of church-building in the 11th century—described so evocatively c.1026 by the monk-chronicler Radulph Glaber (985–1047) as a 'white mantle of churches'—reflected landlords' attempts to provide enduring places of worship, built in stone.

6. Frescoes painted by Maestro dell'Undicesimo Nicchione of the Seven Works of Mercy in the Baptistery of Parma (c.1370–80): 'Giving Drink to the Thirsty' captures both need and the recipients' gratitude

Such lords also appointed the priests, a right that in the 11th century was energetically disputed by the papacy. The intertwining of the life-cycle and the seasons of the year into Christian ritual made the rural settlement a social framework rich in overlapping relationships and meanings.

Collective experiences of work and worship reinforced the bonds of cooperation which were required within any rural community whose members often struggled to survive. Competition existed alongside collaboration. Tensions abounded within and between households: between the young and old, the industrious and the idle, those more or less well-off. There was hierarchy within villages too: with those who owned or held land, and those who did not, with men—who were the tenants of land—and women, who depended upon their male kin. There was also charity and sharing, encouraged by religious instruction (Figure 6).

Cities

Although most people in medieval Europe were attached to work on the land, a significant number were engaged in manufacture and trade, in study, and in the provision of educational and religious services from urban centres. Cities and towns were hubs for the marketing and distribution of agricultural produce, livestock, and raw materials. The marketplace defined the town's commercial capacity, and so in most European cities the great church stood in the marketplace: in Freiburg the church of St Mary still inhabits the marketplace, and in Cambridge Great St Mary's stands just at its edge.

Cities were central to life in medieval Europe. The Roman legacy meant that a city like *Civitas Moguntiarum*, situated at the confluence of the Main and Rhine rivers, remained an important medieval city—Mainz. Its bishops nurtured a buoyant economy—with much vine-growing—and also led in the 8th century the war against the Saxons, and the mission which followed. New cities were created where political realities required them. Magdeburg in Lower Saxony was founded by Charlemagne in 805 after he vanquished the Saxons and forced their conversion. It later prospered as an eastern outpost of the Ottonian Empire. From Magdeburg St Adalbert (d. 981) launched the efforts to convert the Magyars. In the early 11th century its economic importance was recognized by the grant of the right to hold a market. It had already been elevated to the status of archbishopric at the heart of a vast ecclesiastical province.

As economic activity intensified after the year 1000 so did the measures created to secure travel and exchange. Lords secured the freedom of travellers, maintained bridges and roads, and in return exacted tolls. In Italy these common interests between local landholders and cities were identified and forged into a form of joint governance—the commune. In 11th and 12th century communes these interests combined to create political entities as in Genoa, Parma, and Verona. Such cities guarded their liberty, especially regarding their obligations to their overlord, the Holy Roman Emperor.

All over Europe new towns and cities were created by enterprising rulers, bishops, and abbots. In Castile and Aragon royal charters, *fueros*, were issued aimed at encouraging settlement in cities that had recently been conquered from Muslim rulers. The charter for Cuenca welcomed in 1187 'whoever may come to live…whether Christian, Moor or Jew, free or servile'. The kings of France also encouraged urban growth and fostered the vast fairs of Champagne in the 12th and early 13th centuries; the kings of England granted borough status to tens of towns in the 12th century, and the Teutonic Order similarly encouraged city life after its conquest of Livonia in the 13th. But rulers rarely gave up their rights altogether, and continued to exact from cities annual payments, or contributions to their armies.

Those who governed the city sought to create an environment conducive to trade. A safe and healthy city was more likely to attract merchants, who were taxed on the merchandise they imported. Visiting merchants spent a great deal of money in towns and cities on bed, board, and entertainment. City councils regulated prices of food and drink, licensed and supervised sex workers, and guarded access at their gates. International agreements sought to protect such traders as they travelled away from kin and native community. A letter sent by Magnus Håkonsson, King of Norway, to the city of Hamburg in 1264 reassured it that although some Hamburg merchants had been accused of murder while trading in Norway, they were able to prove their innocence supported by the oath of 12 men, and so he set them free. All was well.

The Holy Roman Emperors created in the 13th century the status of Imperial City (*Reichsstadt*), like Regensburg, Hamburg, or Bremen. Imperial officials no longer conducted the cities' affairs, which hence were passed on to the local council, usually dominated by great merchants. The city was now obliged to contribute considerable annual payments for the right to manage its affairs, repair its walls, arm its militia, and regulate its guilds and market. Clashes between imperial cities and the Holy Roman Emperor arose over the treatment of Jews, political alliances between the city and the Emperor's enemies, and on the level of fiscal contributions to the imperial coffers.

Urban centres prospered, diversified, and encouraged creativity. Republican government spawned administration and strategic planning which involved rich merchants above all, sometimes with the participation of traders and artisans. The size of city councils varied from the very small—with seven or eight members—to vast assemblies of hundreds, as in Venice. Time invested in public office was usually given freely, though expenses for entertainment and travel could be reclaimed from the city's coffers. Urban government had to include many of those who produced its wealth, while protecting the aspirations of its richest and most prestigious members. The struggle over representation was incessant, between the rich merchants (often with aristocratic associates) and guild-members. The voice of labourers and women had no official representation.

Cities saw in the 13th century an extraordinary explosion in financial services. Banking dynasties were established and by 1300 they had branches in major European cities. Their wealth made them ambitious within their natal cities, even as they travelled widely and commanded influence abroad. London alone had agents of at least ten Italian banking families, and their financial support underwrote military ventures by the English crown. Merchant and banking wealth was displayed in the building of great residences in Italian and Flemish cities. Kinship loyalty and mercantile acumen combined to create formidable mercantile lineages. The most famous long-distance merchant of the period, the Venetian Marco Polo (1254–1324), travelled to the Chinese court with his father and uncle, Niccolò and Maffeo. Such travel was a form of apprenticeship by which families trained their young in the secrets of trade. In this extraordinary case, the trip lasted 24 years, and Marco Polo committed his experiences to writing.

All the aspirations and the frustrations of a city's life are captured in the story of Siena. Siena emerged in the 13th century from a vast hinterland of viticulture, grain- and sheep-farming as a centre for banking and trade. Siena's precocious textile industry and banking soon followed: wool was turned into fine cloth, metal from surrounding mines into finely wrought weapons and tools. Its merchants and bankers financed and managed the earnings from the seasonal transport of sheep from inland to the coast for sale. When Siena triumphed over Florence and its allies at the Battle of Montaperti in 1260, it entered a period of self-governance—enabled by economic growth. The Sienese rebuilt and extended their cathedral—the Duomo—built the city hall—the Palazzo Pubblico—and decorated the city with religious images.

Siena is situated along a route—the *via francigena*—which linked northern Europeans to Rome. Sienese business and charitable institutions, like Santa Maria della Scala—which can still be seen facing the cathedral—fed, lodged, and cared for these travellers. The Duomo was originally dedicated to the local saints Ansanus, Savinus, Crescentius, and Victor, but by the 12th century was dedicated to the most beloved of all saints—the Virgin Mary.

Sienese artists were much admired for their distinctive style, evident from the late 13th century. Men like Duccio di Buoninsegna (d. 1319) refined painting traditions influenced by centuries of exposure to Byzantine art—with gold backgrounds, mournful and static Madonnas, forbidding crucifixions. Duccio created a style which responded to the civic religion of Siena, to the emotional devotion prompted by the Franciscan friars, creating a distinctive Tuscan style.

A blend of group solidarity and competition animated Sienese life in this period. All year long its neighbourhoods prepared for the summer city-wide horse races, the greatest *palio* on the feast of the Assumption in August. The vast palaces along its main thoroughfare were homes to wealthy families like the Saraceni, Piccolomini, and Chigi. Each was involved in Europe-wide affairs, but each also fostered its local identity through networks of kinship and patronage and a great deal of display. A council of nine men ruled the city for almost a century. It rendered accounts annually in public and ornate documents, and even occasionally brought in monks of the region to act as auditors.

Siena's public spaces help us understand how preaching affected city life. Sienese walls and doorways are still marked with the emblem IHS—*Ihesus*—a logo invented by the preacher Bernardino of Siena (1380–1444), whose fiery preaching we have already encountered. This was an image for devotion, not to the saints but to Jesus. Bernardino was appointed by the Sienese council to preach the reform of morals especially among its super-rich citizens. He used sarcasm, humour, and terrifying images, to lambast gambling, feasting, rich trousseaux for brides, homosexuality, and witchcraft. His pulpit can still be seen today, white marble under a blazing sun, as hot as the man and his message.

Association, guilds, and 'republics'

As the example of Siena shows, competing forms of political and social association developed in cities. Though the gap between the richest and the poorest was vast, cities also saw a great deal of cooperation. This was required by the processes of manufacture and social relations: the production of cloth involved several different crafts working in sequence; neighbours combined to improve their quality of life, ensuring the safety of life and limb. The shared responsibility for maintaining churches and city-walls, and for collecting taxes to support all of these efforts, meant that a great deal of collaboration, scrutiny, and discussion characterized city life.

Alongside the social hierarchy endorsed by kingship and the aristocratic cultures of European landed elites, another tradition developed, which was corporate or consultative, sometimes called republican. It was facilitated by the models of practice of ancient Rome, in the concept of liberty, in traditions of public debate, and in Roman law. The term *universitas*—the very word that begat 'university'—described the corporate entity of individuals with a common aim.

As a *universitas*, the corporate body made up of several members spoke in one voice. A good example is the craft guild in which a city's artisans or merchants combined for the promotion of their economic and political ends. Acting as a guild, they managed to negotiate good prices for raw materials—wool for weavers, wood for carpenters, livestock for butchers—to seek support for beneficial policies with the town council; or to agree the prices of their products or wares. The guild could also set the criteria for membership by the length and nature of apprenticeships, and by exercising control over the quality of its members' work. Guild members were bound by oaths of secrecy and loyalty against all others.

Each artisan or trader was stronger for being part of such a corporate body, and in turn had to obey its rules, pay a membership fee, and respect the prices set—or rather fixed—by it. Elaborate rituals bound guild members and their families, as did the neighbourhood which resulted from the location of a given craft in a single street. Many European streets are still named after them: 'rue des forgeurs' (Smiths' Street) or 'via dei Calzaiuoli' (Shoemakers' Street) bear testimony to the lives passed there in social, religious, and professional cooperation. Guild members habitually sought to marry their offspring to those of fellow members, thus ensuring the continuity of the occupation and its benefits within the family. The feast day of the guild's patron saint—St Luke for painters, St Honoré for bakers, St Eligius for goldsmiths—was celebrated, sometimes in a chapel built by and for the guild. On such occasions, religious ritual and social aspiration combined, as they did at the funerals of guild members, which all were expected to attend. So central were guilds to urban life, so crucial was the contribution of guildsmen to urban finances that in many cities guilds formed the basis for political representation, as delegates from each guild combined into the town council.

The model of corporate existence served many different ends. The inhabitants of the Alpine valley of Saanen (in the modern canton of Bern) combined in the 14th century to negotiate the purchase of their freedom and managed their affairs corporately in subsequent decades. A tiny republic developed in Gersau on Lake Lucerne in 1390, and managed its local affairs through consultation among male householders. Beyond the local, political entities occasionally identified shared interests over vast territories and created associations which adopted the term *Liga*. There was the Lombard League of Italian cities which associated for the purpose of political and military resistance to the Holy Roman Emperor and his allies. It developed in 1167 out of the association of northern cities and came to include members from central Italy too: Verona, Vicenza, Brescia, Milan, Bologna, Vercelli, and more. Memories of the League inspired in the 1990s the Northern league party in Italy, which sought regional autonomy within a federal Italy.

Elsewhere in the Empire association characterized both the urban and the aristocratic spheres. There were leagues of cities such as the Swabian League created in 1331 as an association privileged by freedoms granted by the Emperor, and a bulwark against his enemies. Cities like Augsburg, Ulm, and Heilbronn associated to raise armies and negotiate as a group. Such concerted work required an active bureaucracy with the powers to tax their citizens and conduct diplomacy—and even war—on behalf of member cities. Around 1307 a sworn association of Swiss cities—among them Bern, Fribourg, and Lucerne—joined a group of rural polities to create the Swiss Confederacy of cantons, which continued to grow into the 15th century.

Further north associational ideas became evident somewhat later. A powerful trading association brought together cities of the northern and Baltic spheres: the Hansa. It began as an association of merchants and developed, from 1356, as a league of over a hundred cities, led by the great port cities—Lübeck, Visby, Bergen, Hull—but including river ports deep inland in Germany and Flanders. The League awarded to Hanseatic traders rights in all its member cities. It raised armies, and forced dynasts—such as the King of Denmark in 1370—to allow free passage for its merchants. In the later 14th century the Hansa invested in maritime action against pirates, and negotiated for privileges effectively with the king of England. In this manner the associated cities, whose merchants traded in the 13th century mostly in raw materials of the north—fur, wood, metal ores, amber, rye—also developed a wide range of financial services and perfected the production of luxury goods.

This social and political lifestyle was associational, and autonomous of the dynastic spaces within which it existed. Merchants moved within the Hansa sphere with ease: a Rigan merchant might live, trade, and flourish in Bruges, and a merchant of Lübeck buy a house and raise a family in Bergen, while still maintaining close trading contacts with family members in Lübeck. This was also a cultural zone; parishioners in Bergen and Tallinn (Reval) worshipped in front of altarpieces made by artists from Bruges and Lübeck. The Hansa emphasized the freedom to trade within its sphere, and adopted republican Roman titles—such as Consul—for its officials. Thomas Mann's masterpiece *Buddenbrooks* (1901) captures some of the long-standing aspirations and much of the legacy of the Hanseatic social and economic system.

These types of horizontal associations are evident in different parts of Europe. Rulers sometimes promoted them—as we have seen in the case of the Swabian League—but other times feared and resented them. In 1388 Richard II, king of England, ordered a survey of all sworn associations in the kingdom. He saw in them a means by which wealth could be hidden from taxation, and subversive activities be planned in secret. The returns filed in chancery a year later documented a wealth of sworn groupings—the partial survey yielded over 600 responses—for the most part associations with modest religious and civic aims.

Laypeople in search of enhanced religious experience sought to associate in religious groups, variously known as brotherhoods, *confréries*, *hermandades*, or *Bruderschaften*. As a corporation they undertook collective initiatives: they collected membership fees, elected officials, took oaths of loyalty and secrecy, hired chaplains to pray for the souls of dead members, engaged preachers, had plays and hymns composed for their use, and commissioned artists to paint altarpieces for their chapels. Those who set up such initiatives preferred to join others like themselves—in wealth or disposition—whom they could trust. These corporate bodies sometimes used the language of kinship to emphasize the bond of loyalty and discretion between them.

The habit of association was strong in the European tradition. It was chosen by people of all estates as a mode of interaction which was safe and effective: one voice made up of many. Hence nobles associated in elite orders of chivalry, like the Order of St George, founded by Charles I of Hungary in 1326, or the Order of the Garter, created by Edward III in 1348. Less formal association was also available, for a particular purpose, on crusade or pilgrimage. That is just what Geoffrey Chaucer had in mind when he described a mixed group of pilgrims to Canterbury, a brotherhood for a while.

Chapter 3
The big idea: Christian salvation

In the course of the 14th century the religion born in Judaea, the offshoot of Judaism which for several centuries did not possess a name, became a growing and ultimately defining force—Christianity. Christians were known throughout the Roman Empire, not least for the spectacular, cruel persecutions they suffered under emperors like Diocletian (245–311) and Julian (330–63). Emperor Constantine (c.272–337) made the religion licit, and its tenets were publicly discussed in councils led by him. By the end of the 4th century it had become the official religion of the Roman Empire, replacing the cult of the emperor.

Christianity offered a route to personal salvation within a community of believers, thanks to the saving grace brought to the world by the Incarnation, the birth of God as the man Jesus. The early centuries had seen the emergence of Christian communities in cities around the Mediterranean, founded by apostles, led by bishops, guided in ritual life by priests and deacons. Christianity was alive throughout the Near East, in north Africa, and in large parts of Europe, but its message was universal.

Christian salvation

In Gaul, north Africa, Spain, and Italy, elite men, educated in the classical curriculum, trained for public service and its rewards, became the leaders of Christian Europe. Such men—and women largely within the family sphere—had begun to embrace Christianity in large numbers just as the political order around them was dramatically changing. For centuries the Empire had been sharing territory with barbarian people and their leaders. While defence of the Empire was increasingly handed over to these barbarian leaders, the Roman elite turned in large numbers to Christian leadership: the soldier-saints St Martin or St Germanus, the bishop-saints Ambrose (*c.*340–397) and later Augustine, each offered a model for Christian lives in the world. Senatorial families provided bishops and public servants. Men like Boethius (*c.*480–524) and Cassiodorus (*c.*485–*c.*585) were aware of the political changes affecting their world, under its new rulers. Through public service—which was the traditional vocation of men of their rank—they sought to defend the Christian ethos and Roman law.

Bishops now collected tax income that had once been paid to imperial governors and with it they fortified their cities against attack, ensured regular water and grain supply, built churches for growing communities, dealt summarily with vestiges of pagan worship, established charitable arrangements, and comforted their flocks at times of hardship. Bishop Vilicus of Metz (bishop 542–568) was praised for his foresight in storing grain and defending his city against invasion. A council of 585 instructed that bishops should not keep dogs, who might discourage those in need from approaching them. Bishops supported the aspirations of Christians by maintaining ritual and explaining beliefs, in the cathedral churches and baptisteries which soon adorned every city.

Classical lore had been produced within a pagan world: its poetry exalted gods and goddesses, its law imagined a god-like emperor as head of state, its philosophies offered routes to perfection that were vastly at odds with those of Christian morality. Between 300 and 600, a process was under way of 'Christianizing' that classical tradition. From Spain, we have Prudentius (348–413), lawyer and provincial governor, but also a poet, a Christian poet. He used his exquisite literary and rhetorical training—as befitted a Roman trained in the law—to Christian ends: composing poetry in praise of martyrs, ethical debates about the psychology of sin, and polemics against those who still espoused pagan sympathies. His exact contemporary Augustine attempted a similar—though vastly more ambitious—transformation in his *The City of God against the Pagans*, written after the traumatic sack of Rome by the Visigoths in 410. In this work of history and theology, Augustine reflected on the Roman past and criticized the pagan world view. He also offered an ethical programme Christian to the core, by which sinful humans might live in the world, while aspiring to the City of God. Augustine's work was fundamental to theological and political thought in subsequent centuries; its concepts were based on the philosophy, grammar, rhetoric, and poetics of late antiquity.

These Christian leaders used their education and social clout to celebrate and enhance their religion as it reached new peoples. The poet Venantius Fortunatus (*c.*530–609) provides a good example: he was born to a privileged family in northern Italy, was educated in Ravenna, the Ostrogothic capital, and then travelled north to become a public intellectual in the Frankish court. His poetry was based on the models of Ovid and Virgil, and it extolled Christian dynasts, charismatic abbesses, and devout virgins. Through efforts like his, Christian culture developed outside the clerical sphere and engaged a privileged laity: he composed poems to celebrate royal weddings and hymns for saints' days. He developed hagiographical writing—about the exemplary lives of Christian saints, like Radegund the princess-turned-abbess of Holy Cross in Poitiers—a distinctive new Christian genre.

Cities revered their saints and martyrs, those who had brought Christianity to their parts, some during the period of persecution, martyrs such as Ferreolus of Vienne or Symphronius of Arles. Saint Genovefa (*c*.419–*c*.512)—later known in French as Geneviève—was the well-born daughter of parents who owned estates not far from Paris. She was precocious in her religion, led a devout life from a house in Paris, and from there also encouraged Parisians as they faced attack from the Huns in 451. She was obeyed, admired, and treated as a saint after her death.

The robust and resilient Christian culture of Ireland produced several effective leaders in this period. St Columbanus (543–615), a missionary to recently converted Burgundy, settled with his followers in the ruins of a fort—*Luxovlum*, Luxeuil—with the support of a Burgundian courtier. A pattern of religious life grew there, which was later emulated by other communities. Here was the work of lay patron and religious enthusiast; here too was the implantation of Christian living within a rural setting, and its effect was felt throughout the region.

The extension of Christianity into areas which had had little contact with the Roman world was a greater challenge. The power of Christian rituals had to be demonstrated as true and efficacious. Like all religions, it had to nurture conversations with the dead, and support social relations. A dedicated elite of—often monastic—missionaries travelled from vibrant centres of Christian life to areas of encounter with pagans. The Life of St Barbatus recounts his conversion of the Lombards of Benevento in 663: he chopped down the tree where their rituals took place, dug up and pulverized its roots. Once Barbatus' power—and the impotence of the tree—was demonstrated, he was elected bishop of Benevento by his new Christian flock. So St Boniface (*c*.675–754) travelled from Wessex to Utrecht, to work alongside the missionary Willibrord among the Frisians. On a second journey he travelled to Rome for papal blessing of his mission, and turned to work among the Saxons, in north Hesse at the borders of the Frankish kingdom. The accounts of his life describe feats of confrontation with the sacred symbols of the Saxons, especially when he managed to destroy their sacred oak tree with impunity, a spot where a monastery was later built, at Fritzlar. Like many missionaries he died at the hands of those he sought to convert, on his last mission to Frisia. The Crusaders who attacked in 1168 the temple at Arkona, on the Baltic island of Rügen, removed the statue of the God Svantevit, chopped it up and used the wood to cook their dinner. Or so we are told....

Snorri Sturluson's *Heimskringla* of *c.*1230, a saga which recounts the deeds of the Norse kings, describes how King Olaf (*c.*960–1000) came to embrace Christianity. As a pagan Olaf visited a prophet who lived on the Scilly Islands, only to hear of his own destiny: to baptize and lead many others to the true religion. This later account none the less captures a tradition about the charismatic intervention that turned Olaf into the missionary king of Norway and Iceland. To rulers, like Olaf, who took great pride in their martial leadership and prowess, Christianity had to appear as a triumphant religion, one which would lead its followers to victory in the world as well as over death. And so, the figure of Christ—as represented in word and image—was made to seem victorious and majestic. On occasion the material culture and liturgy of Christianity could impress and overwhelm. So lively was the biblical scene performed to educate the Livs in 1205 that they ran away, thinking that the violence was aimed against them.

While these efforts to spread Christianity continued in the East and North, a religious culture was developing in its reach and impact on European elites from the courts of rulers in whose domains Christianity was securely established. Between 841 and 843 the Frankish noble woman Dhuoda wrote a book of guidance for her son William, recently called to the royal court of west Francia. The work is a love-offering by a caring and anxious mother, but it also shows how central the psalms were to an aristocrat of the 9th century. With hundreds of citations from the psalms, alongside references to Augustine, Dhuoda speaks of those intimate moments when her son prepares for sleep and recommends prayers for his safety. Dhuoda's work also shows that reading developed a sensibility and delicacy of feeling. Such skills and insights are here used by a mother for her son, but were equally useful for a judge in court, as for a priest caring for his flock. Just over a century later in a religious house for women, Gandersheim in Lower Saxony, Hrotswitha (935–c.1002) wrote comedies after the Roman Terence and plays and readings about the suffering of Christian martyrs, among them many women. In a religious house for high-born women, she had excellent Latin, and so produced verses in the metre used by Homer in the *Iliad*. The reach of European Christian culture was such that Hrotswitha and her sisters in Saxony were aware of and felt sympathy for those Christians who had suffered martyrdom in Muslim Cordoba Spain in the 850s; she dedicated a poem to them.

Monastic ideas and practices

The desire to seek salvation through personal hardship and to fight sin in dedicated communities outside the bustle of daily life inspired several experiments in solitary or isolated living, like those of Columbanus. A model for religious life within a community was formulated in the 6th century by the monk Benedict of Nursia (c.480–c.547). The son of a landed Umbrian family, following his education Benedict embarked on a religious quest in solitude, and lived for a number of years in the hills around Subiaco. He founded and guided religious communities in the area, and ultimately led his own monastery at Monte Cassino from 529, along the principles summarized in his Rule. His became an influential vision of Christian perfection, an enduring achievement in religious organization that was soon adopted in hundreds of religious houses all over Europe.

Inspired by earlier experiments in collective religious life, Benedict's vision recommended a balanced life style for sustainable communities. At the heart of the monastic experience was personal striving in a collective setting. The communal aspect meant that no individual could own personal wealth or belongings, nor sustain ascetic devotions unchecked. At the head of the monastery stood its elected spiritual leader, the abbot; like all fathers he guided but also disciplined and punished. The work of God—*opus dei*—flowed in a continuous offering of prayer and collective worship. But there were other tasks to be done—labour—in cellars and gardens, to ensure that food was ready to be taken communally, that sick monks were nursed, and above all that monks were not idle.

Life in the Benedictine house was supported by produce and income from agricultural land, endowments created by founders and benefactors as perpetual gifts. Grateful recipients of miraculous cures at monastic shrines added to a house's wealth. When the lady Ricburgis visited the shrine of St Gertrude at Nivelle in 785, she gained a cure. In return she handed over to the nunnery 12 manors and their serfs, as well as a church of which she was the patron. More modest folk showed their appreciation in other ways. Following cure at the shrine of the boy-martyr William of Norwich, in the 1150s, a 10-year-old boy from the village of Wortham in Suffolk offered himself to Norwich Cathedral priory in service for life.

Administering the monastery involved contact between monks and the outer world: in the supervision of agricultural labour, marketing of produce, entertainment of benefactors, interaction with local bishops, and care for pilgrims in those monasteries which were homes to saints' shrines. These tasks were usually allocated to experienced obedientiaries, office holders in discrete areas of responsibility, while laymen were employed to execute legal and commercial tasks. The intrusion of worldly activities and concerns into the monastery created perennial tensions; it sometimes required that monks abandon the basic principle of monastic life, stability—*stabilitas loci*.

All these difficulties were compounded in the case of female religious houses, for nuns depended on men not only in the field, marketplace, and court, but also for divine office and celebration of the sacraments. Some monastic leaders offered pastoral guidance to women. Caesarius of Arles (c.468–542) composed in 512 a rule for the nuns led by his sister. It emphasized strict enclosure; unlike monks, the nuns were never to entertain religious dignitaries, and could dine only with other religious women. The monk Rudolf of Fulda wrote in 836 a hagiographical text, The Life of St Leoba, and sent a copy to the Saxon nun Hathumoda (840–74), so she 'might have something to read with pleasure and to imitate conscientiously'. In some places 'double' monasteries were created side by side. Indeed, both Columbanus, whom we have encountered in Luxeuil, and Brigit of Kildare (c.451–525), founded such double communities. Influence from Gaul inspired similar Anglo-Saxon experiments: under St Hilda at Whitby, and St Etheldreda at Ely. In all these cases, powerful women, royal by birth or marriage, were involved in the foundations, and their authority and charisma allowed them also to assume leadership within them. The tradition of dual religious houses was not sustainable in the long run, although it had its occasional advocates over the centuries—like St Gilbert of Sempringham (c.1083–1190) in England, or Bridget of Sweden (1303–73). Complaints about abuses prompted bishops and popes to establish different pathways for men and women even within a single order: like the Cistercians, Franciscans, and Dominicans in later centuries. On average, women's religious houses received less generous endowments; hence they were usually smaller and more economically vulnerable.

The Benedictine rule formed the basis for reform initiatives in almost every century. In 910 William, Duke of Aquitaine, granted some woodland to Berno, first abbot of Cluny in Burgundy. Here a religious 'order' was born, with daughters under the leadership of the mother house. Its message was one of incessant and elaborate prayer, freedom from all supervision save that of the pope, within architectural settings of enhanced luxury: with carved pillars, luxurious vessels for the celebration of the divine office, elaborate chant. Cluniac houses attracted aristocratic and royal founders and high-born recruits. They offered a monastic experience for the elite, magnificent and sumptuous.

At the end of the 11th century another attempt at reform developed, when a group of monks gathered around St Robert of Molesme (*c*.1029–1111)—member of a knightly family from Champagne—for an experiment in rigorous monastic living in Cîteaux, in Burgundy. Their vision was not of incessant prayer, but rather of labour. In inhospitable environments, and on marginal lands, the Cistercians sought wilderness as escape from the world. Their quest for seclusion and hard work coincided with the trends of economic growth at that time: the clearing of hitherto uninhabited lands, and the development of more intensive forms of agriculture to feed a fast growing population. Cistercian houses managed thriving farms—granges—under the care of committed brothers and with the labour of lay converts, who were welcomed into the order, in Yorkshire, Tuscany, Wales, Bohemia, and Pomerania. The resulting accumulation of wealth allowed them to develop excellent libraries, and buildings that were well laid out and built. Their innovative recruitment policy, which allowed laymen unschooled in Latin to join as brother-labourers—*conversi*—made the Cistercian Order extremely fashionable and thus popular in the 12th and 13th centuries.

Leaders of the Cistercian movement—for its houses were closely knit and ultimately became an order—sought to enforce uniformity and rigour in all houses by having groups from established monasteries found new ones. And so, Cistercians from Fountains in Yorkshire founded in 1146 the first Norwegian house, at Lyse, near Bergen. Yet it is also clear that each house responded to local religious styles and enthusiasms. The Cistercians of England were among the first to adopt the feast of the new saint Thomas Becket in the 1170s, those of Kołbacz Abbey in Pomerania dedicated a chapel to St Otto, the region's patron saint, while in Scotland, Melrose Abbey maintained a chapel to St Bride. Networks of kinship affected recruitment: early in the 13th century at the Danish house of Løgum the Cantor (in charge of the choir) had a brother among the lay brethren. The Cistercian congregation soon numbered hundreds of houses, with their unadorned churches and simple chant. The most celebrated Cistercian thinker, Bernard of Clairvaux (1090–1153), was a mystic, theologian, and polemicist. He captured the ardour of early Cistercian life, when he lambasted the artworks of other monastic orders. While monks attempted to read the holy scripture they were diverted by the images around them: 'What are the filthy apes doing there? The fierce lions? The monstrous centaurs?', he asked.

It is hard to identify the motivations which led young people to join the religious life, since our sources are often hagiographical in tone, and celebrate the later life of a monastic saint. Some families solved their problems by placing members in a monastic house; some rulers exiled enemies to them. Up to the 12th century it was possible to offer children to religious houses, as oblates—*oblati*—literally, offerings. Thereafter adult consent was officially required before joining. Many worldly folk chose to retire in religious houses, doing penance for lives of sin in relative comfort and security. Some of the attraction may have been in that religious houses were centres of extraordinary activity in education, learning, music, art, gardening, medicine, and all these activities offered possibilities for personal development, while fulfilling a religious vocation. Abbess Hathumoda of Gandersheim in Saxony was described by her biographer-monk as wrestling with her demanding role as abbess: 'She pondered what it meant to be called mother...and desired to be loved rather than feared.' Abbess Hildegard of Bingen (1098–1179) developed a life of leadership, scholarship, mysticism even as she became involved in ecclesiastical politics.

Religious houses were smallish organizations, whose members all knew each other, and yet were diverse by age and disposition. A monastery had its discrete departments: cellar, kitchen, writing workshop (*scriptorium*), infirmary, school, choir; and in these drudgery and accomplishment were combined. Collective practices created great intimacy: some 8th century Anglo-Saxon monastic scribes perfected the ability to write in a distinctive and identical bookhand. Like all institutions, these harboured mean-spirited and bossy people, alongside kind and helpful ones. Away from family and friends, monasteries nurtured deep and passionate friendships as well as jealousy and sad frustration.

Each monastery was also part of a larger network of patronage and cooperation. This was clearest in the case of orders, but it worked through regional networks too. The book created by Herrad of Landsberg, abbess of Hohenburg Abbey in Alsace between 1167 and 1185—the *Hortus deliciarum* (Garden of Delights)—was a wonderful illuminated manuscript of theological, literary, and musical knowledge for her nuns. It was achieved through careful compilation from manuscripts borrowed by Herrad from the neighbouring monastery of Marbach. Intense correspondences bound religious houses and their members: letters were often read aloud by the messengers who delivered them. Monasteries were also bound as associations offering prayers for the dead; St Evroul's in Normandy was associated with 87 other houses for mutual prayer; St Martial of Limoges, with 37. Parchment rolls containing the names of the dead were circulated between religious houses, prompting reciprocal prayer for the souls of the deceased.

Some of the most important debates about the tenets of Christianity took place within and between monasteries. Some of the earliest discussions of the nature of the sacraments, particularly the eucharist, took place between two monks—Paschasius and Ratramnus—in a single monastery, Corbie in Picardy, in the 830s.

In 12th century England monks disputed heatedly the wisdom of celebrating the feast of the Virgin Mary's Conception, an event which is not recorded in the gospels. Polemics developed between monastic orders as every newly founded order criticized the old and established for laxity and abuse. Important new theological approaches and insights flowed from the pens of monks and nuns: the influential formulation which explained why God had to become incarnate was developed by the monk Anselm (c.1033–1109), an Italian monk who became archbishop of Canterbury, in his *Cur Deus Homo*. These debates were expressed with the flourishes of classical rhetoric, citation of biblical authorities, and sometimes developed into impassioned personal campaigns.

Monastic houses affected religious culture far beyond the convent walls. Monasteries became centres for religious writing in the vernacular languages, often for the religious care of nuns. They were centres for the production of works of art. For rural Europeans the most visible representation of Christian life—definitely the most impressive—was a monastery. Religious institutions were relatively long-lasting; they maintained the cults of local saints, occasionally offered pastoral care, and made distributions of food on feast days and at times of need. Recruitment to monasteries was usually local, so networks of landholding and local influence were also invested in these religious houses.

Some of the more notable monastic strivers became so famous that their death inspired expectations of miraculous happenings. When Adelheid of Villich (c.970–1015) of Cologne died away from the religious house for canonesses she had founded, the bishop of Cologne was eager to keep her body in his cathedral, as a focus for pilgrimage and cult. Her sisters managed to secure her return for burial in the cloister grounds, as had been her wish. Yet success bred disruptions; as so many religious houses discovered, the needs of pilgrims and their joyous celebrations disrupted the calm sought by their communities.

The relationship between religious houses and local parishes—once these became established all over Europe in the course of the 12th century—was complex. Monasteries enriched the religious routines of the nearby parish through formal and informal influences. Such exchange was imagined in an instructive tale recounted by the Cistercian monk Caesarius of Heisterbach (1199–1240). A priest of the diocese of Trier spent some time in a Cistercian monastery and learned there the antiphon *Salve regina, mater misericordie* (Hail Queen, Mother of Mercy). This hymn served him well, for when he was caught in a storm some time later and took refuge in a church, he begged Mary to calm the thunder, and was rewarded since he had sung her antiphon so often and with true devotion.

The Church in search of liberty

With the growth of the European economy and the decline of the frequency of disruptive invasions, a more integrated Europe was emerging soon after the year 1000. Recent conversion had brought Iceland as well as Bohemia into the religious and dynastic fold of Europe, Poland as well as Denmark. Migration from the more densely settled west to the east meant that intensive agrarian methods were spread, so more plentiful foodstuff was grown to support growing populations. In many of these activities ecclesiastical institutions—monasteries above all—led the way: they were a relatively stable presence, endowed by members of local elites, and home to recruits from those classes too. Monasteries were sometimes vanguards of political and economic power: when Guifred, Count of Urgel repopulated Catalonia in the late 9th century, he did so with monasteries planted in the plain of Urgel.

Bishops led their surrounding diocese from churches that came to be known as cathedrals, after the bishop's throne—*cathedra*. Most European cities had a baptismal church where the lives of local people became Christian. The most prominent cities—old Roman *civitates*, hence the word city—served as administrative centres for ecclesiastical and secular affairs. Even as other churches and chapels were built at the tombs of saints, these existed in subordination to the baptismal church, the city's mother church.

Despite the influence of religious houses, the occasional support of landed families, and the sporadic inspiration of holy people, provision in the countryside was patchy, and until the 12th century bore little uniformity across Europe. Aristocratic households had their domestic chaplains, and their members were able to found monasteries and nunneries. Landlords built churches on their estates for their dependants; they appointed priests and furnished the needs of the altar. Bishops played an important role in offering centres for training of the clergy in cathedral schools. Before 1000 it was still possible for married men to become priests and to maintain their families.

However far it may have seemed from some of Europe's provinces, Rome was an unrivalled Christian centre. Imperial symbolism was still palpable in the rituals of the papacy: vestments, chant, and titles. Popes promoted not only local Roman saints—the martyrs Peter and Paul, Nereus and Achileus—but also the cult of the Virgin Mary, which had developed early and vigorously in Constantinople. In Rome, Charlemagne sought to be crowned in the year 800. Later German kings sought elevation there too. It was indeed such a Holy Roman Emperor—Henry III (1017–56)—who encouraged the conception of the Church in the world as a hierarchical bureaucratic structure with the pope as its head. Popes—as bishops of the unique city of Rome and vicars of Christ on earth—invested bishops with their office and authority, and these in turn supervised the diocese and all its believers like good shepherds. Or so was the ideal.

The vision now emanating from Rome was one of Church hierarchy and discipline, and of freedom from secular powers—*libertas ecclesiae*, freedom of the Church. Similar ideas had been expressed earlier in the century by the Peace of God movement in northern France, which urged the Church to use its authority to control knightly violence and protect the vulnerable; or by the Pataria in Milan, which protested against the princely clerical dynasties that controlled the prestigious Milanese church. The idea of freedom had been developed in a more limited sense already by the order of Cluny, accountable to Rome alone and to no other secular authority. Pope Gregory VII (c.1015–85) led the reform; he never stopped being the Cluniac monk Hildebrand of his earlier vocation.

The powerful concept of Church liberty, with its roots in Roman conceptions of *libertas*, was promoted by Gregory VII, and it inspired new theological, legal, and diplomatic activity. Gregory sought to make the Church free in its appointments from imperial and royal intervention so as to allow the holders of ecclesiastical offices to act freely, not as clients of great men. The practice of payment for ecclesiastical office—named simony—and of promoting unsuitable relatives to ecclesiastical offices—called Nicolaitism—was deeply embedded, and papal polemicists set out to achieve a major shift in attitude, by deeming it an intolerable abuse. Gregory VII used legates—ambassadors empowered to act in all parts of Europe—to argue the papacy's case and apply it in local contexts.

Such a shift in aspirations was bound to become a political struggle over the authority to appoint bishops, to convene Christian courts, to legislate and correct marriage, to define the ethics of warfare and business, and occasionally—of necessity—to correct rulers. It brought Gregory into conflict with the Emperor of his day, Henry IV (1050–1106), and led to the spiritual leader's use of the ultimate weapon: excommunication of the Emperor from the rituals of Christian life. A dramatic showdown obliged Henry IV to seek reconciliation with the pope in a degrading ritual of penance, at Canossa in 1077. In societies where traditions of sacred kinship had taken root, in which kings were charismatic military leaders who expected loyalty from their men, how was this ambitious new vision of a Christian society guided by its priests to be achieved?

The 12th century saw several similar clashes between rulers and bishops who upheld the 'liberty' of the Church—its autonomy in spiritual matters. The struggle between pope and Emperor occasionally resulted in schisms over the choice of pope. In 1159 Europe's rulers were called to decide which of two popes—both elected by the cardinals in Rome—they recognized: Alexander III or Victor IV. The former, an extremely active legislator and leader, was supported by all but Emperor Frederick I and the imperial bishops. Such dysfunction had very practical results, for during such a schism who was to receive the tithes paid by believers? Appoint bishops? Decide in cases of appeals to Rome?

The papacy's claims came up against the jurisdiction of royal justice, particularly over the legal status of the clergy. On occasion kings acted against bishops in a combination of principle and whimsy. And so, one of the first native Slav bishops of Poland, Stanisław (1030–79), an educated and effective leader, met his death as a martyr at the command of the king he had served, Bolesław II. At issue were a series of confrontations over ecclesiastical property, but also the right of a bishop to chastise the morality of a king. The rift between Henry II (1133–89), king of England, and his erstwhile chancellor, advisor, and friend, later Archbishop of Canterbury, Thomas Becket (c.1118–70), was caused among other issues by disputes over the right to bring priests to court, and the authority of the pope in England. When Becket was murdered in his cathedral the response to his speedy canonization in 1173 as a martyr was vibrant and widespread: Thomas was an English saint, but his story made sense far beyond the English Channel.

Ultimately, kings and prelates developed an accommodation, for rulers depended on the ritual support and the training only churchmen could provide, while Church institutions depended on the protection and privileges which kings alone could assure. And so by the year 1200 dynastic rulers shared jurisdiction over their people with Church courts. In these a vast array of business was transacted: probate, trials for blasphemy and heresy, as well as the all-important business of marriage that touched the lives of all.

Parish Christianity

After *c.*1200 Christian beliefs and practices were disseminated widely and regularly to Europeans in some 90,000 parishes. The parish church became a familiar space over a lifetime of worship—frequent or infrequent—where individuals and families celebrated the most important moments of their lives. In northern Europe churches were built in wood, in its south, in stone, and their ornamentation and furnishings depended a great deal on who worshipped within. Priests and communities shared the responsibility for maintenance of church fabric, but if a rich patron took charge then a parish church might acquire magnificent paintings, a bell tower, a fine altarpiece and—after 1000—some statues, and later decorated windows too. Parish churches were beautified with the handicraft of their people: the embroidered cloths for the altar made by women, or the careful maintenance of fabric by men. How well the parish functioned and how much it offered in religious education and spiritual consolation depended on the parish priest, his training and motivation, and on the vigilance of the bishop to whose diocese it belonged. Bishops aimed to provide helpful manuals for the struggling priest, model sermons, and lists of questions to guide confession. Townspeople benefited from variety in religious services—in parishes, guild-chapels, and cathedrals, indoors and out—offered by preachers and religious teachers with sermons and religious drama.

Many of these arrangements were transformed between 1100 and 1200 through concerted efforts of bishops and secular rulers (Box 2). A system of parishes now prevailed, some based on long-standing arrangements for provision of pastoral care. Each

Box 2 The Fourth Lateran Council

Pope Innocent III (1160–1216) spent over two years planning this ecumenical—world-embracing—council. In November 1215, 412 bishops, 900 abbots, and many representatives of secular rulers gathered at the papal palace in Rome, for discussions over the next three weeks (Figure 7). These resulted in some 70 determinations—canons—which addressed central aspects of religious life, with special attention to provision for lay people in the parishes, and the correction of heresy. In the decades that followed bishops legislated on the basis of these canons, in their local synods, and so spread a shared blueprint for Christian life all over Europe. The Council made important and lasting provisions: it made belief in transubstantiation an article of faith and established the requirement of all believers to attend confession and receive communion every year. The Council also required that Jews and Muslims wear a distinguishing mark on their clothing, so as to discourage mixing with Christians; and called for a new crusade to the Holy Land.

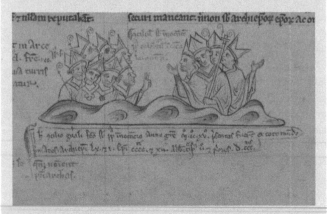

7. The English monk-chronicler Matthew Paris depicts the heated discussions at the Fourth Lateran Council of 1215, where a wide programme for Christian life was promulgated

parish was a unit of liturgy and bureaucracy, of discipline and the payment of tithes. Parishes across Europe ranged from small and numerous, such as those of a city like York, to vast and rural, as found in Pomerania and Livonia. Parish Christianity was a combination of ritual, instruction, participation, and contribution by the laity under the guidance of priests, and from *c.*1250, with the help of lay churchwardens too.

The parish church was many things: a meeting place, a safe-haven, a storage space, and a ritual platform. Important points in the life-cycle were associated with church rituals, and were celebrated within parish churches or near them: birth, coming of age, marriage, and death. The Church's great treasure—saving grace—was conveyed by priests to parishioners through the sacraments. Baptism erased the stain of original sin (Figure 8), which was passed on to the foetus at conception, and created spiritual companions—godparents—who committed themselves to support the new Christian. At puberty the Christian's faith was confirmed with a boost of grace conveyed with the touch of blessed aromatic oil—chrism—from the hand of a bishop; from then on the individual combated sin with the aid of annual confession and the penance that followed (Figure 8). Marriage was undertaken for the creation of Christian households and to aid the bridling of sinful desire.

Every adult was obliged to confess annually and perform the penance enjoined by the priest, all in preparation for deserving reception of the bread consecrated at the altar during the mass—the bread which was thus transformed into Christ's flesh and blood, in a process which came to be named transubstantiation. The Saga of Pál Jónsson (1155–1211), Bishop of Skálholt in Iceland, recounts that he deemed the mass so momentous a sacrament as to replace the need for frequent preaching. At the end of life, as they faced the uncertain journey beyond death, the sacrament of extreme unction was administered, the last boost of grace, offered by

8. **Lorenzo Maitani's carving on the façade of Orvieto cathedral, (c.1310–20) depicts the scene of Adam and Eve's temptation**

a priest at the deathbed. It was preceded by confession
and communion, and took the form of anointing with holy
chrism.

The parish served not only the living, but also their dead. Care
for the dead was traditionally the responsibility of families.
Frankish and Visigothic laws supported the dignity of the dead
by severe legislation against grave robbers. With the rise of
the parish, the dead were remembered in all services, and parish
priests offered guidance in preparation for death, which could
occur at any moment. While holy people went to paradise and

9. Carving of c.1110–50 above the portal of the Abbey of St Foy in Conques, vividly depicting the joy of the elect on the left, and the suffering of the damned, on the right, as they enter the mouth of Hell

evil ones to hell (Figure 9), most folk probably understood themselves—and their loved ones—as belonging to neither category. Parish instruction was guided by developments in theology, and saw the introduction around the year 1200 of more precise teachings about Purgatory. This was a place of cleansing—purgation—through suffering and anguish, at the end of which the purged person merited a place in heaven. The length of time spent in purgatory could not be known, and so people were encouraged to gather as much merit as they could—through prayer, good works, and, indeed, prayers on their behalf after death by priests and well-wishers—and hope their suffering would thus be mitigated if not avoided altogether. As in so many cases, the rich could indulge their anxiety and also express their devotion to dead loved ones, by setting up elaborate arrangements for prayer in their lifetime or leaving instructions for such in their wills: in chapels and chantries, and by establishing charitable institutions whose poor generated grateful prayer. Ghost stories often told of a husband returning from the dead to his widow, to admonish her for failing to provide the prayer for his soul set out in his will.

The parish encompassed all areas of life, from cradle to grave. Alongside its planning and provision for a ritual life that matched the complexities of human experience, the Church enforced a regime of truth and scrutiny. Throughout the 12th century it developed techniques for searching the conscience in preparation for confession. The more generic and often public penance of the earlier centuries gave way to probing of circumstance and intention in judging an act: who? what? where? through whom? when? how many times? why? The discipline engaged a vast bureaucracy in its church courts, in visitations of parishes, and in special courts charged with seeking out and correcting heresy, the papal inquisition. Heresy, the 'queen of mistruths', clearly required treatment by torture, 'queen of torment'. The use of torture was rare, and disciplines most frequently worked through the fear of banishment from community life. The sanction of excommunication—being set outside communion with Christians—meant that a person thus punished could not receive the sacraments, or participate in church services. It was meant to force people to admit their guilt, repent, confess, and do penance. An interdict was another form of discipline, pronounced against a whole people, usually in order to coerce a ruler to papal will. And so, it was imposed on England between 1208 and 1213, following King John's refusal to accept the pope's appointee as archbishop of Canterbury. In 1376, the city of Florence was placed under interdict during its territorial war with the papacy, so the Florentines drilled holes in church walls in order to observe the services being conducted within religious houses.

Beyond the parish

Those who could not afford to join a religious institution could pursue the route of seclusion as solitary hermits in woods, on mountain tops, in remote uninhabited places. This was an option open to men alone, since women's lives were supervised by men. Yet a few women were able to live in seclusion within their communities, immured close to parish churches, in cell-like dwellings, as anchoresses.

For the more sociable, pilgrimage was an exciting pathway towards cure and penance. While the rich and powerful could travel to those places intimately associated with the Christian story, like Rome and Jerusalem, most people visited their local shrines. Visits to sacred places—be they the tomb of saint or martyr, or shrine for the veneration of a relic—inspired a travel literature which allowed the experiences of the few to reach many more. By the end of the 8th century the *Einsiedeln Itinerary* described for Frankish audiences several trajectories across the city of Rome, while in later centuries a 'virtual pilgrimage' experience was enabled by altarpieces and prayer books which allowed enclosed religious none the less to imagine themselves in the holy places.

The scheme for salvation offered by the Christian Church was based on intricate blending of belief with the practices of daily life. Throughout our period there were those who saw Christian life in the world as too lax, and the Church as too much involved in worldly affairs. Periodic movements of reform sought to remedy this tension. It was sometimes the very individuals most engaged in the world who became its greatest critics. The merchant of Lyon, Valdès (*c*.1140–*c*.1218), gave away his riches and preached poverty to the laity with his band of male and female followers, later known as Waldensians. Francis of Assisi (*c*.1181–1226), son of a rich merchant of Assisi, lived the privileged life of a young man in an Umbrian city, but turned to the gospel of poverty in the midst of commercial wealth and civic ambition. Franciscans created a new—and initially alarming—form of religious life which flew in the face of the emergent parish system. They did not initially receive ordination, or serve a parish, but were free agents whose lives offered an example and their preaching, exhortation.

They lived as beggars and preached in the local languages. So remarkable was its possible contribution that this counter-cultural movement was authorized by the papacy as its very own secret weapon in the struggle against apathy. By licensing the Franciscans and seeking their loyalty Pope Innocent III (1160–1216) invited the harshest critics of religious 'business as usual' into his tent. Hundreds of friars' convents were created all over Europe, supported by the laity. Their arrival in Denmark may be typical: a group of barefoot Franciscans entered the town of Ribe in 1232, and the town gave them a house; over the next few years friaries were built in several other Danish towns, and endowed by secular benefactors.

It is not surprising that parish priests and bishops resented this intrusion. If people preferred to attend the services offered by the new arrivals, what was to become of the parish as the focus of religious experience, and as the recipient of laypeople's support? The parish priest was a consummate multi-tasker: he celebrated the daily office, visited the sick, cared for the needy, managed parish property, instructed the young—while the friars were specialist preachers. The orders of friars supported their members during university study with comfortable residences and libraries, and also trained their members in hundreds of convents all over Europe (Figure 10). They provided Europe with some of its most influential thinkers, among others the Franciscan mystic and theologian Bonaventure (1221–74), and his exact contemporary, the greatest medieval theologian, the Dominican Thomas Aquinas (1225–74), and the greatest scientist of the age—expert in astronomy, optics, and more—the Franciscan Roger Bacon (1214–94), the possible inventor of spectacles. Like most charismatic movements, the friars developed a less demanding lifestyle over time. In turn, satirical treatment lampooned friars and their ways, as did Geoffrey Chaucer in his pilgrim Friar, described as 'wanton and merry', full of gossip and 'fair language'.

In the earlier centuries of our period, much cultural discussion and production took place in monasteries or in courts. With

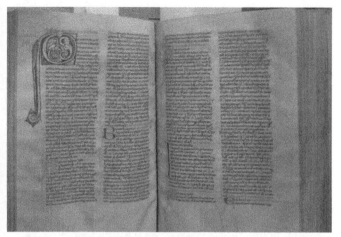

10. Bible, probably from Oxford (*c*.1250)—a new type of book for the use of scholars, like the Dominicans for which it was made. It is portable, clearly laid out, and easy for reference

parish religion and the sacramental life-cycle new qualities influenced religious experience. One of the most apparent is the attachment to the Virgin Mary. The imperial cast of majesty given her in 5th and 6th century Byzantium, a style adopted in the court artists of the Carolingian and Ottonian Empire as well as by Anglo-Saxon artists, was transformed over the 12th century into something new: the Virgin Mary as a mother at home, engaged with her son, at work, prayer, and play. Moreover, the humble supplications which monks had developed over the centuries were now spoken in all languages, from Hungarian to Provençal, Icelandic to Catalan. The Mary experience was accessible, and it resonated with life as most Europeans knew it.

The drama of salvation penetrated the parishes in sermons, artworks, and liturgy. The devotion which exalted the crucified Christ and fostered sympathy with the suffering God, born in the monasteries of the 11th century, was now a message for townspeople too, through the preaching of the friars. Francis himself exhibited unique identification with Christ by receiving five telling wounds—mirroring those on Christ's body, on his two hands, two feet, and on his side—the *stigmata*. Believers were encouraged to identify with the sorrow of God, and of his grieving mother (Figure 11), and some went so far as to devote their leisure to the re-enactment of this compassion: in religious clubs dedicated to reciting devotional poetry, some accompanied by self-flagellation. As believers were drawn to a heightened sensibility to the Crucifixion during Lent and Holy Week, the difference between Christians and Jews was sensed most viscerally, prompting abuse and violence.

The involvement of lay people in religious activities was particularly noticeable in cities, where there was great wealth, and where the

11. This Sculpted group by Niccolo dell'Arca for Santa Maria della Vita in Bologna *c.*1462/3, conveying the emotional intensity which became associated with the contemplation of Christ's Passion, and which Christian audiences were invited to explore

fostering of civic activities was at the core of existence. We have seen how central shared rituals were to a city like Siena. The participation of lay people as religious agents was now widespread, and it allowed women to become more visible too. Among the saints canonized after 1250 there are many more lay people, and many more women. And among those who were just admired in their communities were married women, widows, women of no learning, and visionaries. In the cities of the Low Countries and north Germany groups of women—beguines—combined manual labour in textile or lacemaking with charitable works, forming something like a parish unto themselves within a bustling city. Several assemblages of buildings—*beguinages* or *begijnhoven*—like those of Bruges and Ghent still convey the sense of order, modesty, and calm created by these busy religious women. They attracted suspicion and displeasure from some, but several far-sighted bishops and confessors understood how inspiring such women could be.

European regions bred their own versions of religious identity. The cities of Flanders and Italy, where the gap between rich and poor was so stark, and where the mutations of worldly fortune were particularly acute, produced a gospel of radical poverty. The region of Languedoc in southern France with its distinctive Occitan culture, as well as some parts of northern and central Italy, received by the mid-12th century a brand of religion which we may call dualist, and it came to be known as Cathar. It espoused a cosmology in which two principles—one material and passing, the other spiritual and lasting—were at war.

Cathars rejected the sacraments which infused matter with grace, and recognized but one ritual act, the *consolamentum*, received by the most perfect Cathars. Cathars were led by the preaching of 'good' men and women, towards disassociation from flesh, sex, and power. The king of France and the pope combined in an attempt to bring Languedoc into the kingdom of France, and Cathars into the Catholic fold, in campaigns that have come to be known as the Albigensian Crusade (1209–29). As the northern army commanded by Simon IV de Montfort (1165–1218) confronted those of the Count of Toulouse, thousands were slaughtered in Cathar strongholds, like Béziers and Carcassonne. The Cathar religion was largely destroyed, but its beliefs still permeated Christian life a century later. The dualist tone of the villagers of Montaillou attracted the bishop of Pamiers' inquisition between 1318 and 1324, and the resulting trial records contain the most detailed testimonies about these often complex religious beliefs.

Once lay people became involved in the making of religious life, it was impossible to contain the habit of inventive public religion. This was most evident at times of great distress. The response to the Black Death (1347–52) came in the form of many new associations: burial societies, flagellant associations, and novel arrangements for commemoration of the dead. Anyone who could afford it aimed to amplify the provision of prayers for themselves and their loved ones. Initiatives that called for Church reform took many different forms. In Bohemia a sentiment of ethnic identity was channelled into resistance to a largely German-speaking clergy. Inspired by the university theologian Jan Hus (1369–1415) a widespread movement—the Hussites—sought political independence from the Empire, and reform of the sacraments. In consequence, Hus was executed and the Emperor led a crusade against the offending region.

Although a priest was always required for the celebration of the sacraments, lay people—ranging from rich merchants to artisans, including men and women—sometimes preferred to go it alone. Some enriched their lives with books and images to hand, with regular access to a favourite preacher, or through connection with a religious house. In Flemish cities the Modern Devotion bypassed almost altogether involvement with the clergy, as its members concentrated on good works, reading of the Bible and devotional writings, while still remaining active in the world. Demand for devotional images, generated by this knowing laity, encouraged artisans to create the first engravings, and then a few decades later, the first woodcuts, the fledglings of the print revolution. By the early 15th century it was possible to buy strips of religious images, mechanically reproduced engravings, and these were sometimes hung on walls, or sewn into prayers books, especially those of religious women.

In Italian cities the 15th century saw an interest in the religious inspiration offered by children. Religious companies for youths, like the Company of the Archangel Raphael founded in Florence in 1411, displayed the purity and innocence of the young in processions, and enjoyed their musical performances. At the very end of our period the infamous charismatic preacher Girolamo Savonarola (1452–98) managed to infect Florence in the 1490s with religious enthusiasm, and employed youths in penitential processions, aimed at chastising sinners. On Palm Sunday boys and girls processed dressed in white, olive branches in their hair, and crosses in their hands. Renaissance Florence was clearly attuned to some very traditional modes of religious experience, which cannot simply be assigned to practices of the 'Middle Ages'. Savonarola was hanged and burned as a heretic in 1498, a sign of the volatility and diversity of these styles of religious devotion and their political resonances.

Chapter 4
Kingship, lordship, and government

Sacred kingship

We have already observed the dynamic blending between the legacy of Christian imperial rule, and the charismatic martial lordship which prevailed among Germanic people. This process resulted in the emergence of sacred kingship as a concept and a practice. It caused the aspirations of dynasts to merge with ideas of justice, mercy, and rule by the grace of God. This was a challenging blend which intellectuals strove to inculcate and which powerful men struggled to fulfil.

After their conversion to Christianity, barbarian rulers adopted imperial ritual and symbols. Such leaders of confederations of kin groups were magnified into Christian rulers. By the year 800 Charlemagne demonstrated that a king could even claim the title of emperor. And by the year 1000 the concept of *beata stirps*—blessed root—was developed by writers in the Ottonian court to describe that lineage. Writers of epics and romance in later centuries imagined that those born to rule carried a special mark on their skin.

Sacred kingship was born of a pact between dynastic rulers and the church. The church shared the expertise and service of its highly trained personnel with the ruler, and offered its counsel in spiritual matters as well as rituals of sacred power. In turn, rulers were expected to preserve Christian identity, protect the church, and promote justice and peace. Such relationships were often forged through the process of conversion. Stephen, born to the Hungarian Christian Grand-Prince Geza, embraced the possibilities of Christian rule. He defeated remaining pagan rulers in the region, and with the blessing of Pope Sylvester II was crowned king in 1000. He learned how to rule as a Christian from his wife, Gisela (985–1065), herself a daughter of the Duke of Bavaria and of a Burgundian princess. Gifts, and ecclesiastical endorsement secured such dynastic marriages. The couple promoted Christianity in Hungary through legislation and example, and embraced above all the cult of the Virgin Mary. Stephen's new status elevated him above other nobles in the Carpathian region. Similarly, King Valdemar of Denmark confirmed his new status as sole Danish ruler in 1170 by a gathering of his nobles—*Landsthing*—confirmed by ecclesiastical anointment and coronation.

As a new Christian dynasty was formed family traditions of sanctity often followed. Veneration developed around Vladimir, king of Kievan Rus' (*c.*958–1015), enhanced by the treatment of his sons Boris and Gleb—who died at war—as martyrs. Traditions of royal piety often ran in families. St Elizabeth of Hungary (1207–31) was married at 14 and widowed by the age of 20, when she turned to the service of the sick for the rest of her life. Her niece, Margaret of Hungary (1242–71), was raised in monasteries and was dedicated by her parents to the religious life.

When Duke William of Normandy invaded and conquered large parts of England in 1066 and its aftermath, he too became a sacred monarch. With papal approval he was crowned in Westminster Abbey by Ealdred, archbishop of York, in a scene memorably captured by the needlework of the English women who crafted the Bayeux Tapestry. In this role William espoused church reform, as an early adopter of the new papal ideas about church freedoms. He allowed church courts to flourish even as he developed his own sphere of secular legislation. The church, in turn, assisted the process of Normanization, and provided the kingdom with its educated class of royal ministers and advisors.

Sacred kingship is probably best known to most readers for its pomp and its legacy of visual art and music, architecture and ceremony. St Vitus' Cathedral in Prague, with its chapel of St Wenceslas, is still home to the crown jewels, so close to the formidable royal castle. The images and actions of Christian kingship were adopted through dynastic contacts. When Richard II, king of England, married Anne of Bohemia (1366–94), daughter of the Emperor Charles IV, in 1381, his court learned from her imperial courtiers. The Westminster Portrait, a unique image of enthroned majesty, now in Westminster Abbey, reflects in its frontal austerity traditions Bohemians had acquired from the Byzantine East. Against a gold background, the king is seated with sceptre and orb, crowned and vested, unlike any English ruler before him. In a set of panels also commissioned by Richard II, the Wilton Diptych, the spiritual and religious dimension are explicitly bound: on the left, Richard kneels with a group of St John the Baptist, King Edward the Confessor (1033–66), and St Edmund (d. 869) behind him. The whole group faces the Virgin Mary surrounded by her heavenly court, and her son hands the banner of the Resurrection—symbol of sacred power—to the man destined to rule.

Since sacred monarchs were expected to use violence in the promotion of Christian peace, they seemed to be the natural leaders of religious warfare. Some answered the call more eagerly than others, but all were obliged to respond. The armed pilgrimage to Jerusalem which came to be known as the First Crusade (1095–9) was led by European aristocrats. But by the second crusade (1145–9) both Conrad III (1093–1152), king of Germany, and Louis VII (1120–80), king of France, were drawn in as leaders. Richard I (1157–99), king of England, Philip II Augustus (1165–1223), king of France, and Emperor Frederick Barbarossa (1122–90), came together to lead the Third Crusade (1189–92), following the fall of Jerusalem to the hands of Saladin in 1187.

As the power of Christian kingship became well-established during the 11th and 12th centuries, most royal courts settled in capitals, just as Charlemagne had in Aachen centuries earlier: Winchester and then Westminster for the kings of England, Paris as the capital of France, Krakow the new capital of the Poles under Casimir I (1016–58), and Huesca of Ramiro I (by 1007–63), king of Aragon. Even when sacred kings favoured one location as their capital, travel did not cease. When the English royal entourage travelled to campaigns in Scotland in the late 13th and early 14th centuries, several departments of state still functioned from Westminster, but the all-important archive and a great deal of personnel journeyed with the king.

Capitals were designed to reflect the responsibilities and dignities associated with Christian rule: justice, education, and patronage of the church. They became repositories of relics and stages for rituals of state: reception of diplomats, processions on feast days, celebration of victories. Louis IX (1214–70)—who was canonized soon after his death—had the Sainte Chapelle built as the architectural reliquary for the remains of the Crown of Thorns, which he acquired as a gift from the spoils of the sack of Constantinople in 1204. The chapel's Gothic magnificence resounded with the music of a boys' choir, the king's own singers. Similarly magnificent was Westminster Abbey, rebuilt by Henry III; its dynastic narrative emphasized continuity since the days of Edward the Confessor, and a universal Christian loyalty to all things Roman, down to the mosaic pavement which Italian artists laid down in front of the altar in 1268.

Sacred kingship was aligned with effective provision of justice and securing of peace, and rulers were reminded of their responsibilities by a specialized literature—Mirrors for Princes—and by sermons. Some kings gained lasting recognition for their initiatives. King

Alfred the Great (849–99) resisted the Vikings and developed a hegemonic position for himself as king of Wessex. He created a court that was as effective in defence and in raising taxation, as it was in communication with the papacy and European leaders. The achievement that impressed his contemporaries greatly was the commissioning of works aimed at raising the competence of courtiers and clergy. Under Alfred Christian classics like Pope Gregory the Great's *Pastoral Care* and *Dialogues*, Boethius's *Consolation of Philosophy*, Orosius's *Histories against the Pagans*, and Bede's *Ecclesiastical History of the English People* were translated into English. These diverse genres were all aimed at enhancing purpose and horizons among lay and ecclesiastical leaders. And since history supported identity, Alfred most probably launched the *Anglo-Saxon Chronicle*; an inaugural copy was sent out to several monasteries to be kept and updated, in some cases well into the 12th century.

Lordship

In the kingdoms which succeeded the Roman Empire, men who held public offices were often rewarded with entitlement to tax income from land, the *beneficium*—benefice. This system remained largely in place even under the barbarian kings, as it ensured continuity in the functioning of military and administrative staff. In Iberia the Visigothic kings had kept on the Roman treasury—the fisc—which grew as it acquired the confiscated lands of traitors, the possessions of erstwhile temples, or the property of those who died without heirs. In the towns and cities of old Roman provinces, local councillors—*curiales*—continued to collect taxes and pass them on to governors, in a system of administration that was of very long standing. Kings used the system to reward loyal followers, but the benefice was still seen as a public good. And so, in 675, King Theuderic III confiscated the lands of a duke who joined his enemy. Under the Merovingian dynasty of Frankish kings, lands in Gaul were held in this fashion in return for service, and reverted to the king once that service ended. Even under

Charlemagne and his successors, offices were not inherited, and close scrutiny meant that local officials in regions far from the heartland were still understood as servants of the Carolingian 'state'.

All this was tested when in the 9th century Carolingian unitary rule was turned into several kingdoms—east and west Francia, Italy—and with the disruption and violence caused by Vikings, Magyars, and continued Muslim raiding. Public administration faced severe challenges, as local administrators were required to provide fortification, law, and order. Officials went about the work of government as before. In the absence of the close scrutiny which had been in place since *c.*800, the distinction between the public and private good—and property—became blurred, and ultimately disappeared. Counts now passed their office on to their sons, and treated the *benefice* as the means for support of power and authority which ran in the family. They apportioned parts of the lands and income to their followers, as *fiefs*, in return for loyalty and support. The fief supplied the resources for the livelihood and lifestyle of a warrior, the mounted knight, with a warhorse and all equestrian trappings. The punch of military force was now delivered by fighters trained to ride with stirrups, by knights, dextrous with sword, shield, and lance.

This system formed the basis upon which long-term reorganization of land, wealth, and power took place in Europe around the year 1000. It produced a relatively stable ruling class: the royal vassals of the 9th are discernible among the counts and castellans of the 11th century. Such lands formed the basis for independent influence, alongside responsibilities and obligations. By the 11th century the sense of family and lineage around such men and their patrimony was very strong, and it inspired the new genre of family histories, accounts of great deeds, like those of Fulk le Réchin (1043–1109), count of Anjou, of Prince Bolesław of Poland (1086–1138), or the deeds of the Counts of Barcelona, composed between 1162 and 1184 (Box 3). These vassals could

Box 3 Chivalry

The word chivalry—*chevalerie*—describes an array of ideas, practices, and experiences. It was a code of behaviour and a lifestyle for free men engaged in military conduct. Its conventions promoted honourable behaviour in warfare, reciprocal discipline even between enemies, such as in the treatment of prisoners. Chivalry was affected by Christian values, as churchmen aimed to limit the reach of violence: protecting the unarmed, prohibiting violence against religious houses, forbidding warfare during Lent and on religious festivals. It aimed to regulate warfare between members of a warrior class, who might encounter kinsmen in battle, and spare them the worst brutalities of physical mutilation and dishonour. Hence chivalry developed a language of symbols—shapes and colours—which helped identify a knight in armour—and so heraldry was born. Campaigns against Muslims helped strengthen the link between Christian service and warfare, and produced in the 12th century chivalric heroes such as Richard the Lion Heart and El Cid. The rich British historical traditions about King Arthur were rewritten by clerics into poems of knightly endeavour and adventure—like the 'Quest for the Grail'—first in French and then in all other European languages.

Alongside the theme of idealized male valour and loyalty, a fitting form of love developed: courtly love. It imagined the unfulfilled yearning of a knight for a lady of refinement and distinction, and inspired poetry, song, and visual imagery. Chivalry was practised during war, but was also perfected during times of peace in jousts and performances of prowess in courts of great kings and aristocrats. The culture of chivalry was promoted in courts, where women could participate in it as patrons, and take part in the artistic rituals. Immersion in the culture of chivalry led young men of high birth to seek fame and experience in battle: the future King Henry IV (1367–1413) of England joined in his youth the Teutonic Knights on their campaigns to establish Christianity in Livonia (Figure 12). Chivalric themes continued to inspire social relations and artistic production even after the age of the mounted knight gave way to that of mercenaries and cannons.

12. Castle at Malbork (northern Poland), built by the Teutonic Order in 1274, dedicated to the Virgin Mary. It and the town around it reflect the military and political domination of the Order in northeast Europe

become very mighty in turn. The Duke of Normandy—vassal of the king of France—conquered and became king of England; Robert Guiscard (c.1015–85), the sixth son of a Norman noble in Lombard service, became Duke of Apulia and Calabria, and the pope's vassal.

Once it was conceptualized and established, the language of fief, lord, and fealty was written into charters and reflected in law. It also inhabited the world of poetry and history. It was spread and mediated by the educated clergy who helped convert and also administer the new Christian polities. As regions became integrated into Europe, it mixed with indigenous ideas about leadership, valour, and loyalty. A good example is the Norwegian commonwealth—the *Norgesveldet*. The language of lordship and fealty—homage—was used there to express the relationship between Goðrøðr, king of the Manx and Hebrides, and Ingi Haraldsson, king of Norway. Similarly, in 1217, King Logmaðr of Manx and Hebrides was said to hold his kingdom 'in fief' from the king of Norway. In turn, when the Norwegian invasion of Scotland failed, the resulting Treaty of Perth of 1266 reduced the king of Norway to the status of vassal to the king of Scotland, for the Hebrides. By the 13th century dynastic diplomacy had developed as a form of communication and dispute resolution between Europe's rulers. Rulers shared assumptions and the language of lordship with their vassals, and their vassals' vassals, and thus an aristocratic political culture was formed.

The traditions of Roman law prevailed not only in the old Roman provinces, but formed the basis for legal study in courts and schools in the 12th century, as we shall see in a later chapter. Many areas of life—land tenure, marriage, punishment for theft and murder—were regulated by traditional customs—Welsh, Irish, Saxon, Frankish, Alemann, and more—but Roman law was particularly useful for the facilitation of commerce, and its support for the notion of a state and its ruler. Between 1000 and 1200 royal administrations—gradually and not always consistently—worked to remove the treatment of major offences from the sphere of family retribution to that of royal justice. A great deal of arbitration between families meant that not all cases reached the royal courts, but officials sought to identify capital cases for the crown, and mobilized communities as informants—with the requirement to raise the hue and cry—when evidence of a crime was discovered.

Local traditions were subsumed within hegemonic royal legislative systems, like those of Henry II in later-12th century England, or of Alfonso X 'the Wise' of Castile in the mid-13th. Delivery of justice was a royal duty but also an opportunity to exercise power and collect revenues. Royal judges of various titles and capacities travelled throughout the kingdoms to dispense justice. Together with local elite men who provided regular policing and local advice, who empanelled juries and arrested suspects, capital cases were tried—murder, robbery, treason, and more—by royal officials who also collected the resulting fines and punitive confiscation of property.

In the later part of our period we witness royal courts become increasingly elaborate and complex institutions. They legislated on economic affairs, and intervened in commercial activities by controlling the coinage. In England scrutiny of the lucrative wool trade meant that customs were imposed on the 35,000 sacks of wool exported to the Continent in the early-14th century. As kingdoms became larger the burden of military defence and domestic administration became more onerous; they required elaborate central organization and record keeping. The buoyant economy of this period was increasingly complex as a source of income to be monitored through customs and protectionist laws. With so many participants in economic and political life occasions for broad consultation became necessary. The Roman precept 'whatever touches all, must be approved by all' (*quod omnes tangit ab omnibus approbari debet*) animated calls for representation in discussions about fiscal matters, alongside the established consultation between the king and his nobles on matters of war. While lords always had their vassals around them for advice and support, the very greatest lords—kings—required expert advice in finance, law, administration, and diplomacy. This was achieved by the appointment of expert royal servants, but also through consultation. Parliament, *parlement, diet, cortes, landsthag,* developed all over Europe, assemblies aimed at representation that included constituents of the political nation: nobles, churchmen, knights, and townspeople. The broadening of consultation meant that by the 15th century cities were incorporated into the processes by which kings were elected in Poland, Bohemia, and Hungary.

Kings were looked to as patrons for great projects. We have already seen how closely related Christian kingship and leadership of Christian military campaigns became: crusades to the Holy Land, Reconquista in Iberia, and the war against heretics. In the 15th century new horizons for royal patronage similarly invoked royal leadership. From the 1430s the kings of Portugal led the exploration of Africa, providing privileges and charters to official navigators and cartographers. By the end of our period their Iberian neighbours, Ferdinand and Isabella, were approached with a project of commercial enterprise and millenarian enthusiasm: Christopher Columbus' plan for a westward journey to the Indies. Where other monarchs rejected the unprecedented venture by the Genoese trader-traveller, these monarchs retained Columbus and supported him. His vision appealed to their sense of mission and leadership as Christian monarchs.

Chapter 5
Exchange, environments, and resources

We have already discussed natural resources and their uses in this book, but let us consider them again as an economic system of production and exchange. For in our period hard work produced food and raw materials which sustained the population at most times, but which also formed the basis for manufacture, exchange, and trade in luxuries. So, for example, trade linked Scandinavia and Hungary in the 6th century, for we find exquisite northern amber jewellery in burial in women's graves some 1,000 kilometres away from their source. Most regions aimed to produce their own staple goods, so traders transported more exotic goods like ivory, spices, and silk. An 11th century German poem, the *Merigarto*, describes the priest Reginbert earning great riches by selling wine and honey in Iceland. In Norway's oldest monastery, founded at Selja *c.*1100, mass was celebrated by priests dressed in vestments made of Spanish silk.

This high-value trade depended on the availability of a limited stock of silver coinage, centuries after the disappearance of the Roman imperial gold coins. Some of that gold had been turned into treasure—in artefacts related to rituals of church and court, like crosses and crowns—and some ended up in the Muslim world, as payment for goods imported into Europe. In rural society before 1100 there was little use of coinage. New gold coins were minted again only in the 13th century, first by Emperor Frederick II in 1231.

All economic activity was accelerated after the year 1000. Over the next two centuries the sufficiency of foodstuffs and growing populations allowed, as we have seen, for economies, communities, and life styles to become more diverse. Silver finds allowed the money supply to penetrate rural markets and encourage exchange even in modest surpluses of agricultural produce, and so a proliferation of small markets and new towns followed. Trade in basic foodstuffs developed, so that Baltic grain fed Flemish townspeople, allowing some 10–15 per cent of Europeans to buy their food rather than to grow it. New forms of enterprise grew in urban centres: family companies, joint-risk companies, sleeping partners in support of a merchant, all allowed trade to develop, and its effects were to be felt everywhere. Italian merchants led trade with the Far East, while Italian bankers provided the large-scale finance kings required to support war efforts. By the 15th century family-based banks with branches all over Europe were not uncommon: like the Borromei of Milan, who from 1434 had a branch in Bruges and soon after in London too.

Arable and pasture

However diverse the economy it always depended on a rural base. A balance had always to be struck between arable cultivation of fields, and other forms of production in vineyards, pasture, and meadows. The challenge faced by most individuals and communities was the production of food that was suitable and sufficient to meet the needs of working people and livestock, as well as of urban populations. Alongside the production of food was the need to gather, mine, or grow raw materials for the making of clothing, shelter, household goods, and some manufactured goods for luxury markets.

Fields produced grain that was made into the staple foods of bread and porridge. Wheat for the making of white bread was a cash crop rarely eaten by its producers, who consumed rye bread or a bread of mixed grains. Porridge was a staple in many versions: oat-based in Scotland or polenta in central Italy made of barley meal. Such staples were accompanied by much smaller portions—perhaps but a fifth of all intakes—of meat, fish, vegetables, and dairy. When peasants ate meat it was usually beef in Hungary and the Low Countries, fowl in most of France, pork in Germany and the British Isles, mutton and goat in the Mediterranean regions. Sheep milk was used more than cow milk, and sheep-folds were enriched by deposits of manure. Nutrition was enhanced by the drinking of beer: the brown and bitter Celtic and Saxon beer produced by the fermentation of oats, and further north and east, the lighter, barley-based, Germanic beer. In the south young wine was drunk in the growing areas devoted to wine-growing (Box 4).

Box 4 Wine

Although vines could only be cultivated in some parts of Europe—in the Rhine and Mosel valleys, southern France, Iberia, and Italy—wine was enjoyed more widely. Most contemporary wine-producing areas had been identified by Roman times, and viticulture continued there in following centuries. After c.1000 demand for wine grew from northwest Europe, and so the wine trade became a lively sector of the medieval economy. Enterprising bishops—like Rüdiger, archbishop of Speyer in 1084—invited expert wine-growers to settle on their domains and to trade in wine from their cities. Creating a new vineyard was a labour-intensive, and hence expensive, enterprise—involving digging terraces on hillsides, planting to a right angle so as to capture the sun, waiting three years for plants to become established, and requiring constant pruning and care. Great landlords and religious houses were best positioned to become successful wine-makers; peasants were allowed to use their lord's winepress only against payment.

Wine was probably a sourer and weaker drink than that which we drink today, and it was occasionally flavoured with honey, peppers, or cinnamon. The rich could enjoy the fine wines of Cyprus and Gaza, but the habitual wine drinking documented in monasteries, courts, and cities was of younger wines and in great quantities. The hospitality and cuisine of the rich used and displayed wine and every parish church was obliged to use it in its central ritual, the Mass.

The 7th and 8th centuries saw the introduction of the heavy plough to large parts of central and northern Europe. It was usually led by horses—though in England oxen pulled ploughs well into the modern period—each harnessed with a collar for effective control, and supported by metal horseshoes. This plough was able to penetrate deep into heavy soil while turning and breaking it. Such preparation was particularly conducive to the growing of spelt—especially in the northeast; oats and barley, so useful for the feeding of horses, grew even on poor soil and in cool temperatures, if deeply planted. Horses in turn also served as useful draught animals for harrowing and for carting of produce to market as the economy became more commercialized.

These innovations explain how population was able to grow, as it did in some regions from the 9th, and more so from the 10th century. Although yields were paltry compared to rates in modern agriculture, there was still more food available for humans and livestock. The expectation of secure provision of food allowed some people to choose work away from the land, or in specialized occupations in rural areas: ironwork, charcoal making, or estate management. It also meant that country dwellers were able to spend more time on improvement of homes, roads, and drainage in their communities.

At the beginning of our period hunting animals in woods for food and skins, and fishing in streams made a great deal of food available according to season. But with the development over time of more intrusive management of resources by landlords—kings, abbeys, or knights—these resources were more closely controlled. Wood for the building of shelter was readily available in northern Europe, but was increasingly managed as a resource supervised by stewards, and exploited for the highest commercial returns.

Most estates were made of a section of prime land directly exploited by the landlord—the *demesne*—while the rest was divided among serfs. The open fields were cultivated in strips and a single holding was often made of several such strips, each of differing quality and distance from the settlement, so as to ensure equitable distribution. By-laws devised by village communities aimed to ensure mutual support: they often reserved gleaning rights for widows and the poor, food for free. Landlords strove to maximize their income from agricultural cultivation, and so their interests could both coincide and oppose those of their serfs. Projects of clearing and extension of cultivation into new areas—of woodland in Yorkshire, of marshes in the Po valley—saw investment by landlords and settlement of serfs on cleared lands. Fencing and earthworks for the defence of livestock and humans were similarly projects initiated by lords and realized with hard labour on the part of serfs and labourers.

Lordship and legal status shaped the countryside. There were share-cropping arrangements in Iberia and in Italy, which were economically very burdensome, but which did not entail loss of freedom. Such arrangements often existed between the peasant and an ecclesiastical institution, as evident from 10th century charters in northern and central Italy. There were many freeholders in northern and eastern England, and in the newly settled lands of Pomerania and Livonia. In areas of greater commercialization dues owed by serfs were often commuted to cash payments, and these meant that peasants had to participate in exchange—of produce or of some family labour—in order to earn coin. By the end of our period serfdom ties became weaker in western Europe, with many peasants entering fixed-term arrangements with their landlords. The opposite was true in central and eastern Europe.

Demand for agricultural produce came not only from local populations, but was generated from further afield by large concentrations of rich populations, such as cities and courts. The Île-de-France, the hinterland of Paris, marketed its wine and beasts almost exclusively for sale in the capital. By 1300 regions across the south of England tended their woods, raised their beasts, and grew vegetables to supply the demand generated by London's markets. Around that time aristocrats, bishops, and abbots invested in city residences: the abbot of Cluny's palace in Paris is now the *Musée national du Moyen Age*; that of the archbishops of Canterbury in London is Lambeth Palace, on the south bank of the Thames.

After the collapse of demand for food following the catastrophic Black Death landlords chose to move away from arable and to exploit other resources: fishing, mining, hemp growing. Highland areas were much affected by this change, with new investment by landlords: in Wales, Catalonia, the Massif Central, the Apennines, and the Pyrenees. Such change often resulted in more intensive fencing and enclosure, to the detriment of rural working communities.

Woodland

The production of food-grains in fields was but part of the busy and diverse agrarian economy. Fields and woodlands combined to create sustainable habitats for humans and animals. While woodland is often imagined as thick and dark, and so it was in parts of Scandinavia and northeast Europe, large sections of woods were active and noisy. There was constant collection by men and women, young and old, of undergrowth, ferns, gorse, fallen branches of all sorts, to be burnt for heating and cooking, or used in thatching, fencing, basket-making, and construction. Woodlands should be imagined as dotted by clearings and often co-existing with other forms of cultivation. They required a great deal of managing: with coppicing, and growing trees to the size required in construction. The roofs of cathedrals show just how strong and large was the timber that a carefully managed wood could produce.

For centuries scholars have imagined that with the decline of Roman imperial rule Europe 'reverted' and yielded to the forest. This fits well with the view we discussed above of the period 400–600 as one of decline and loss. Yet the combination of archaeology and historical botany now produces a more nuanced picture. With less state-driven demand for wood for construction and public works, management and use of wood was transformed by local communities—and sometimes assisted by legislators—into enterprises aimed at sustaining livelihoods. As demand for food by city dwellers declined some fields were allowed to turn into woodland. Similarly, when state-backed exploitation of mines ceased, as in the Tuscan Maremma, woodland grew over old pits. Chestnut trees were introduced in large parts of Italy, a tree rich in its offerings: excellent building material, good wood for charcoal, and delicious fruit which could be eaten and also made into bread flour. Alongside apple, pear, and walnut, it was considered to be central to human nutrition.

Relations with woodland developed at different speeds across Europe. Around the year 600 the villagers of Prato Spilla in the Apennines cleared areas of forest in order to grow hay instead. Since this upland wood was covered with snow in the winter, they must have used the clearing for grazing only during the spring and summer. Clearing by fire was speedy, but also dangerous and wasteful. So King Lothar I legislated in his capitulary of 840 against starting fires in wooded areas, and threatened to punish those who did with beatings and humiliating head-shaving. Clearing with axes was slower but safer.

In the midst of the woodland areas there was industry too, including charcoal-making and metal work. Wood that did not burn well or safely in domestic fireplaces—like the highly tannic chestnut—was turned into charcoal. Smiths exploited charcoal to make the hot fires required for work in metal; only in later centuries did the smithy become part of the village settlement itself. Demand for charcoal grew particularly in cities, where it was considered safer than the use of branches and faggots. Webs of lordship affected the viability of living off woodland: chestnut groves in Campania were habitually held between 800 and 1000 under agreements that required 1/3 of the yield in chestnuts to be paid to the grove's owner.

As we have seen, demographic growth after the year 1000 saw the rise in demand for food. Larger urban populations had to be fed, and so the extent of woodland was reassessed by landlords. Woodland was increasingly regulated, and by 1200 large tracts were controlled by laws that set them apart as forest—*foris*, outside—for the exclusive use of the lord. Kings, religious houses, and secular landlords, all strove to regulate their woodland, and their efforts spawned a vast officialdom of foresters, woodwards, *verdiers*. By 1300 the king of France was served by a group of Masters of Waters and Forests (*maîtres des eaux et forêts*).

The management of the wooded environment paid attention to sustainability and to commercial profit. It also set aside spaces for leisure and entertainment, hunting for sport being the chosen pastime of aristocrats and their followers. Hunting and trapping was a regular activity to rid estates of foxes and vermin, but hunting with birds and dogs was the privilege of the rich and leisured. Hawking and falconry required long training and expertise, and were discussed in treatises all over Europe, from Wales to Mallorca. The birds were rare; the Teutonic knights caught, trained, and sold gerfalcons to aristocratic households throughout Europe.

Yet there were always woodland areas so marginal as to remain untouched by administration and sport. These became haunts of the imagination that also attracted an alternative social scene in many parts. Fictional accounts of encounters with wild beasts or fantastic individuals may not have been utterly fanciful. Forests were homes to bears, wolves, foxes, and wildcats. Mares lived there during pregnancy and were left there to nurture their foals. The forest drew those who sought to retire from the world—hermits—but also those who sought refuge from the law. One of Europe's most loved heroic figures—Robin Hood—was imagined in refuge in Sherwood Forest.

Water and waterways

Water is essential for all aspects of life: drink and food, industry, and hygiene. In old Roman provinces people still benefited from public works associated with water supply: aqueducts, baths, conduits, and canals. Churches often had fountains in the entry courtyards—*atria*—a welcoming aspect rich with symbolic value signifying life and purity. Streams offered water for washing, but domestic supplies were often engineered for the use of cities, and on large estates. As in so many areas of life, these traditions were maintained by bishops and public officials in the early part of our period: pope Hadrian I (700–95) maintained the Roman aqueducts, and a century later the bishops of Le Mans still tended to those of their city. Religious houses led the way in maintaining the quality of water as they did in other aspects of domestic material culture: bishop Rigobert of Reims (d. 743) provided piped water for the canons of his cathedral and in the Flemish village of Kootwijk each household had its own well *c.*1000. Bathing was uncommon but people regularly washed their faces and hands. By the 12th century Cistercian abbeys led the way in the exploitation of water for domestic use: the model which characterized the order's houses always situated the monastery along a river, and sewage was carried away from latrines situated over the moving water. They also spread the use of waterpower for the grinding of corn grains and for fulling (where woollen cloth is beaten by wooden hammers).

Europe is well-served by its rivers. North to south and east to west, it is linked by rivers on which cargo and people travelled easily. The Baltic grain that fed Flemish townspeople made its way along the Vistula, and inland river ports formed links with sea ports, like Norwich and Yarmouth, thus allowing both centres to flourish. A river ran through every great city. Think of Paris, London, Cologne, and Rome. Many bridges stood on Roman foundations. Florence's Ponte Vecchio did, and also housed more recent structures, butchers' stalls built of wood, which were on occasion swept away by floods. Building bridges in cities—like the Charles Bridge in Prague, which began in 1357—were prestige projects initiated by rulers.

Rivers spelt danger too. Through the rivers of Europe, east and west, the Vikings penetrated into England, France, the Baltic lands, and deep into modern Ukraine in the 9th and 10th centuries. Any invading force—like the English during the Hundred Years War—could reach Paris easily from the coast. Rivers flooded regularly; when the Danube did in 1194 this was a disaster in Austria for both humans and their livestock. People stumbled and fell into rivers, like the boy depicted in a 15th century English manuscript, driven into the Thames by a herd of cows. In eastern England and the Low Countries there were elaborate arrangements for the distribution of responsibilities for maintaining flood defences and irrigation channels. This Flemish expertise was applied in northern Germany and Poland, as new settlements developed there too.

In the countryside access to rivers and their resources was regulated by seigneurial authority: some sections were kept private for the use of lords and their households, and others were open for their dependent tenants. Fishing in rivers was a source of livelihood and subsistence for some, but it was also a business. Fishing rights were managed by rulers as a resource: Desiderius (d. 786), king of the Lombards, handed such rights to his favourites; Carolingian officials protected the right of the monks of Farfa (central Italy) to their fisheries in 798; an association of fishermen in 10th century Pavia negotiated its rights with the king.

Some fish travelled between sea and river—like the salmon—and netted weirs were set up by landlords to capture them at crucial stages. The season and the Christian calendar imposed a rhythm too: throughout Lent, and on Fridays throughout the year, Christians abstained from eating meat. And there were unexpected gifts from the sea. The *Laxdaela Saga*, written down in the 13th century, describes life in Iceland favourably compared to that in the Hebrides: there were plenty of beached whales there—a sole whale could feed a family over a whole winter—and it was rich in fish, especially salmon.

Chapter 6
The 'Middle Ages' of 'others'

European cohesion was facilitated by the system of communication—along rivers, roads, and coastlines—and by the increasingly pervasive culture of Christianity. Its presence affected the landscape—cathedrals seen by travellers from afar, especially in northern Europe, once the lofty Gothic prevailed; the presence of individuals in habits or in penitential chains on European roads; the soundscape with processional chants and the ringing of bells; and even the smell of cities (during Lent the smell of roasting meat was absent from city streets).

European identity depended on what it rejected just as much as it did on what it affirmed. So fears and anxieties, objects of hate and disgust form part of this history too. Christian teaching offered a message of hope through redemption, a path to salvation. Those outside the Christian body were destined to live in sin, a menace to themselves and to others. The Carolingian theologian and courtier, Hrabanus Maurus (c.780–856), described pagan gods as demons, who 'even persuaded people to build temples...and to set up altars to them, on which they should pour out for them blood both of animals and even of men'. Through Christianization previous social customs were substituted, but also partly incorporated. The first generations after conversion often sought the co-existence of pagan ways with Christian rituals.

The Hungarian leader Géza (d. 997) converted to Christianity in 972 and obliged his people to do so, but he also continued to 'sacrifice both to the omnipotent God and to various false Gods'. As we have seen, his son Stephen (d. 1038) ruled as king of Hungary from 1000, and was revered as a saint for his commitment to Christianity and his devotion to the Virgin Mary.

In most regions of Europe, for some part of our period, Christians were at war with non-Christians. Differences between groups evident in patterns of kinship or customs of eating and dress—polygamy, eating of prohibited foods—combined with violent encounter to produce a strong sense of 'otherness'. These perceptions were captured in poetry, paintings, polemic tracts, and chronicles. The Paris-educated priest Gerald of Wales (c.1146–c.1223) wrote four works about the strangeness of the Irish and the Welsh, who seemed barbarous and incomprehensible, at the borders of the civilized Anglo-Norman polity. The encounter between Christianity and Islam was powerfully represented in the heroic epic, probably as old as the event it depicts—the Battle of Roncevaux in the Pyrenees, of 778—known to us from 12th century manuscripts: the *Chanson de Roland*, Roland's Song. In it, Charlemagne and his men confront different Muslim types—bold Muslim emir, wise advisor, female convert to Christianity—and enact feats of often foolhardy bravery. A literary tradition of border ballads and miracles tales exploited the themes of Christian–Muslim military rivalry, up to the 15th century and the fall of the last Muslim stronghold, Granada, in 1492.

Yet not all otherness was experienced at borders, or confronted through military encounters. A Parisian chronicler described the arrival in 1427—in the midst of the fair at St Denis, north of Paris—of a group of dark skinned, black haired, exceedingly poor families. This is the first mention of the nomadic groups whose origins may be in Gujarat and who are variously called gypsies, Egyptians, Bohemians, or *gitanes*.

The relationship between Christians and Jews in Europe was old and complex. Jewish life was based on the holy texts that Christians also revered as the Old Testament. These Hebrew texts—translated into Latin in the late 4th century by St Jerome (*c*.347–420)—provided Christians with prophecies that foretold Christian history: the Sacrifice of Isaac prefigured death on the Cross, the Burning Bush offered an image for the unsullied virginity of Mary. Augustine saw scripture as a bond between Jews and Christians, and argued for toleration of Jews within the Empire, as living testimony to Christian truth and future converts at the end of time.

Jews lived in Roman cities, where they witnessed the rise of Christianity. When Barbarian rulers issued law codes for their Christian kingdoms, they sometimes included clauses about Jews. The Visigothic rulers of Spain wove attitudes to Jews into dynastic politics. Recarred tolerated Jewish presence in 589, but his successor Sisebut introduced harsh economic restrictions on Jewish labour and livelihood. King Recceswinth required, in 681, that Jews convert or go into exile: 'whoever he may be, shall have his head shaved, receive a hundred lashes, and pay the required penalty of exile. His property shall pass over into the power of the king.' This legislation was overturned a few decades later following the Muslim conquest of Iberia, and the relative toleration of Jews and Christians it introduced.

By 1000 economic and urban growth attracted Jews from southern Europe to settle along the rivers Rhone and Rhine. There they worked on the land or as artisans, workers in metals and textiles. New ways of thinking about Jews developed in these centuries, in the centres of learning where theological debate was intense. As the ambition and reach of Christian institutions grew, so it became increasingly clear which people stood outside the *societas christiana*. When the armed pilgrims on their way to 'liberate' Christ's tomb in Jerusalem passed through the cities of the Rhineland in spring 1096, they deemed the Jews to be 'killers of Christ' and massacred hundreds.

In the many new monasteries and in cathedral schools the basic Christian concepts were debated: *'Cur deus homo?'* (Why was the incarnation necessary?) asked the monk Anselm, later Archbishop of Canterbury; 'Was Mary, mother of God, touched by original sin?' asked Odo of Cambrai (1050–1113), bishop of Tournai in northern France; 'What is the role of intention in the judgement of human action?' asked the maverick Parisian teacher of philosophy Peter Abelard (1079–1142). The Jew was a privileged sparring partner for those who thought most deeply about Christianity: versed in scripture, yet resistant to the allure of Christianity.

Such debates led to polemics with the Jews, who denied the Incarnation, rejected the notion of Virgin Birth, saw belief in the Trinity as a form of idolatry, and were puzzled by the sacramental powers of water, bread, and wine. Their views were submitted to polemical treatment, sometimes alongside Muslims and pagans. The Cluniac monk Peter the Venerable (*c.*1092–1156) wrote works against Jews, Muslims, and Waldensian heretics; Peter Alfonsi, whom we have already encountered, against Muslims and against Jews.

Outside the intellectual realm, thinking about Jews took place within royal and aristocratic courts and in bureaucratic circles. Dynasts benefited from the unique legal and economic control they had over Jews, their dependants. In large parts of Europe Jews were encouraged to offer credit and to lend against surety. In a charter of 1244, Duke Frederick of Austria defended a Jew's right to secure a pledge forfeited by failure to repay and promised to defend such pledges for the Jew 'against violence'. The kings of England and France placed their Jews under the protection of sheriffs and seneschals so that Jews could prosper and in turn share their profits with the king.

Kings were also amenable to other considerations and influences: the complaints of influential aristocrats, indebted to the Jews, who would see them expelled, or worse; or, from the early 13th century, pressure from the dynamic new branches of the church—like the Franciscans and Dominicans. These preachers sought to animate religious commitment among lay people, often by re-telling dramatic versions of the Crucifixion. This participatory piety pitted Jews as 'killers' of God and enemies of contemporary Christians. New narratives were invented in which Jews were accused of child murder and ritual abuse of Christian sacred objects. Feeling was particularly heightened during Holy Week, with its frequent preaching, public processions, and religious drama.

Rulers vacillated between the lobbying of friars, who often served as personal chaplains and confessors to royals, and the desire to maintain law and order in their domains, while benefiting from the services rendered by Jews. In turn, Jewish leaders pleaded, offering gifts as sweeteners to avert expulsion or abuse. Policies towards Jews thus differed greatly from one reign to another according to the character of rulers and the challenges they faced: Henry III of England was highly active in his attempts to convert Jews, and his son Edward I ceded to the pressure of knights and churchmen to expel the Jews from England in 1290. In 1304 the Jews were expelled from France, only to return and be expelled again in 1394. King Peter IV (1319–87) of Aragon protected Jewish communities, which helped finance his Mediterranean wars, while his son John (1350–96) favoured unfounded allegations of sacramental desecration brought against them in the 1370s.

Following the accusation of well-poisoning levelled against Jews during the Black Death, expulsions became more frequent. The movement of Jewish settlement in the 14th and 15th centuries matched that of political refuge and economic opportunity, from western Europe eastwards, and this led to the creation of large communities in Bohemia, and Poland-Lithuania. The most dramatic transformation in the conditions of European Jews occurred in the century that ended in their expulsion from Spain in 1492. Urban violence in Iberian cities in the 1390s led to mass conversions of more than 100,000 Jews. These 'new' Christians were made by the water of baptism, yet Christians avoided marrying into 'new' Christian families and continued to harbour suspicion towards these *conversos*. The tensions were so acute that the kings of Castile established their own local inquisition, with the task of investigating *conversos* denounced as secretly still harbouring sympathy with the faith of their ancestors. This fault-line of mistrust became so acute that Ferdinand and Isabella—the Catholic Monarchs of a united kingdom of Castile and Aragon—ordered the expulsion of the Jews from the kingdom.

In this manner a global diaspora was created. The Jews of Spain were received for settlement in north African emirates, by the Ottoman rulers, and in Italian cities. They maintained the language of Spanish Jews—*ladino*—a European vernacular which soon became a global one. A few decades later the expulsion of Muslim converts—*Moriscos*—followed.

Even in their absence, in regions where they were little known—like Scandinavia—or in countries from which they had been banished—like England after 1290—Jews were ever present in the European imagination: in the narratives of Jesus' life and the life of his mother; above all in depictions of the Crucifixion. The Hebrew Bible was present at every Christian service, in the Psalms that guided Christians through joy and tribulation. A combination of hatred, fear, and fascination characterized the relationship of Europe with its most intimate, neighbouring 'other'.

Chapter 7
The 'Middle Ages' in our daily lives

As we reach the end of our journey, let us consider some of the legacies of the 'Middle Ages', ones we take for granted.

Universities

As we have seen, learning was wide-ranging and diverse—in cathedrals and courts, in monasteries and urban schools—and it owed a great deal to the Roman curriculum of the liberal arts. The integrated study of rhetoric, logic and grammar, arithmetic, geometry, music and astronomy, provided the basis for understanding the world and its affairs, and for describing it. Cathedral schools attracted students, individual teachers did too, and the 12th century saw a further specialization in centres of learning under the auspices of emperors, kings, and popes.

All Italian cities of that period had some schools which trained notaries. Schools at Padua, Salerno, and Bologna offered professional training in medicine and law from at least the 11th century. Great schools attracted students from afar and their needs inspired the development of the format of the university. The schools of Bologna were granted a set of privileges by Emperor Frederick Barbarossa in 1155, by which they became a *universitas*. This allowed students—mostly foreign students, who sought to ensure their safety and value for money during the years of study—to form a guild of sorts. This chartered organization supervised the terms and quality of teaching and decided the level of payment for teaching.

The University of Paris emerged in a different way. Since the early 12th century, the cathedral of Notre Dame, in the capital city of the kingdom of France, had become a famous school for the liberal arts. Not far from it, on the left bank of the River Seine, a number of important schools also attracted famous teachers and throngs of students from all over Europe. The most famous was Peter Abelard, who perfected the method we call dialectic: an analytical probing of philosophical propositions through formally discussed oppositions. The intellectual environment was fruitful, and so was the ambition of the French crown: to enhance its capital city with schools just as it did with trade. Philip II (1165–1223) of France authorized the creation of a *universitas*, an association of teachers licensed to regulate the lives of students too. Papal endorsement for Paris in 1231 established it as 'parent of all knowledge' (*parens scientiarum*), and a preacher described it later in the century as 'the mill in which all God's wheat is ground for the nourishment of the entire world'. It was famed above all for its arts degree, which imparted the fundamental texts through lectures followed by dialectical disputations, and for its preeminence in theology. And so Paris attracted students from all over Europe whose differences in lifestyle and rivalries led to the organization into four nations: French (central and southern France as well as Iberia), Picard (northern France and Flanders), English (England, Germany, and Scandinavia), and Norman (including Brittany).

Schools existed in many English cities from the 11th century, but for the best higher education, English students flocked in the 12th century to Paris. After King Henry II banned English students from studying in Paris in 1167, many English, Scottish, and other northern students settled in the Oxford schools, and from 1209 in Cambridge. Papal bulls made each a *universitas* a few decades later.

The university enjoyed recognition of its degrees as providing a licence to teach anywhere in Europe. Universities offered the highest training—to doctoral level—in medicine, church (canon) law, and civil (Roman) law. They trained those who became the officials of states and cities: diplomats, judges, tax collectors, and prelates of the church—bishops and even popes. Here again we witness an institution which depended a great deal on long-standing traditions of city life and education, and whose basic curriculum depended on study of the classics.

The arrival of thousands of students animated university towns, with the demand for accommodation, food, and books. Students lived in halls run by private individuals or, in the case of monks or friars, maintained by religious orders. In the late 13th century, a variation on a Parisian invention was introduced: the university college. Colleges began as charitable institutions to support poor students through higher degrees. Endowed by the founder, each college had a library, dining hall, dormitory, and chapel. The community of scholars studied, ate, prayed—and often misbehaved—together. The most famous of these colleges is King's College in Cambridge, founded by Henry VI in 1441 for the training of clerks for the royal chapel. Its world-famous choir still inhabits the chapel, a vast edifice where grateful scholars prayed for the welfare of their benefactor's soul.

From the mid-14th century the link between the demand for trained personnel by state administrations and the location and shape of universities became more explicit. Demand combined with the prestige associated with the patronage of learning. And so, Emperor Charles IV (1316–78) founded Prague University in 1348, and Casimir III (1310–70), king of Poland, founded the University of Krakow in 1364. Princes followed suit, with universities to serve their regions: Galeazzo II Visconti (c.1320–78), ruler of Milan, founded the University of Pavia, in 1361, and the move of the University of Florence to Pisa was organized by Lorenzo de Medici in 1472.

In southern Europe, universities were civic and professional bodies with a mixed clerical and lay membership, in contrast to northern Europe where they were ecclesiastical institutions. In northern universities, whose students and teachers were in clerical orders, the papacy attempted to control the content of teaching and occasionally intervened as censor. Even ancient works could be affected: in 1210 some of Aristotle's scientific writings were condemned, and in the 1270s attempts were made to prohibit certain propositions from debate—like 'That God does not know things other than himself'—under the pain of inquisitorial investigation for heresy. But, like most assaults on academic freedom, these efforts were ultimately unenforceable. It was, indeed, from the new university of Wittenberg in Saxony, founded in 1502, that Martin Luther's (1483–1546) new interpretation of Christianity was spread, initiating the momentous Reformation of European religious life.

University teaching was delivered in lectures, where professors commented on a core text: in geometry, rhetoric, philosophy, or theology. Illuminations to manuscripts show the classroom with its ranks—very much like a modern lecture hall—with the familiar array of avid note-takers alongside bored students, or those deep in conversation. Graduates with a Bachelor of Arts (BA)—today still known by the same name—from the University of Paris or Oxford could expect appointment to a parish living, a teaching or tutoring job, a post in royal administration, or in the service of a city council. Theirs were the skills of communication and recording: drafting letters, keeping official archives, or composing sermons. A few continued to the higher degrees of law, theology, or medicine, which held the promise of high ecclesiastical office, private practice, or membership in a royal or princely entourage. Access to posts depended on patronage, and some graduates waited years for permanent placements. Old boys' networks operated, creating pathways into professions already trodden by friends or relatives. Then as now university years were a time for hard work and hard play. Music and violence, sexual experimentation and satire, all arise intermingled from our sources. Students appear perennially poor, and developed a knack for writing heart-rending letters to friends and patrons in search of support. They drank a great deal and sang a lot too.

In universities the culture of scholarship and the culture of youth met. Friendships made at that formative stage served men in later life. The uniformity of the basic Latin training for the BA meant that educated men all over Europe shared a professional language as well as intellectual habits and tools. These could be very practical: a familiar style in composing letters, favourite moral fables from antiquity known to all, or the manner of approaching problems and seeking solutions to them. This uniformity characterized educated men well into the 19th century. Once women and other less privileged people entered higher education, once the democratic politics of the 20th century questioned the structure of university curricula, and the demands of scientific teaching transformed the teacher/student relationship, the legacy was bound to be transformed, as it has been in most modern universities—transformed, but not out of all recognition.

Universities led some young men to leave their homes and regions, to live in penury and make do with odd jobs—as scribes, secretaries, chaplains for hire. Students benefited from skills and connections which were highly transferable and useful in a wide variety of careers. To become a student they required some support from a patron—a local bishop, landlord of the estate on which they were born, or a well-to-do relative—but many students were poor and unsure of their future prospects. The most distinguished people in society did not send their sons to universities, yet universities were full of bright and lively young people. Even those who dropped out after a year or two had sufficient training to allow them to earn a living. What has not changed is the culture of young adulthood fostered in these institutions of learning, and the possibilities for social mobility these afforded.

Printed books

Even though so much of our reading is now done on screens we still love books, and will no doubt continue to do so. The book format is one of the most remarkable inventions of our period. The ancient world used inscribed surfaces: clay tablets and the easily erasable wax tablets. Greeks and Romans also used scrolls made of durable soft materials, like papyrus in the dry Mediterranean regions. But the codex, or book—with pages that can be leaved—was an invention associated in particular with the spread of Christianity.

The book came to represent Christianity, a religion based on scripture, old and new. Some of the central figures in the Christian tradition are habitually represented by them holding a book: the evangelists—Mark, Matthew, Luke, and John—or Augustine, a father of the Church. Books came increasingly to be used for the preservation and use of scripture, in liturgy and in private devotion. Gospels were some of the prestigious gifts offered to rulers at the moment of conversion—like the glorious St Augustine Gospels—associated with the mission sent from Rome to England.

Books were useful and laden with symbolic meaning. Before the year 1000 most books were to be found in the libraries of monasteries and cathedrals, and in the treasuries of courts. Such courts were often itinerant, and moved between sites according to the season of year, and so important books were transported in chests, and cared for by chaplains. They were protected and respected by the use of expensive bindings, made of ivory, precious metal, or fine leather, and often encrusted with gems and pearls. The contents of books were frequently read aloud: in monastic refectories during meals, in aristocratic halls during feasts, by chaplains in private chapels. Books were rare even towards the end of our period, and the medieval invention of print would change the ubiquity, visibility, and accessibility of books forever.

Those books associated with religion or with the entertainment of the rich and leisured were often decorated lavishly. The 13th century manuscript of the miracles of the Virgin Mary made at the request of Alfonso X (1221–84), king of Castile, contains the text in verse, in the courtly Galician, inscribed on pages which were also heavily decorated with illustrations of the text as well as by notes for singing it. Far less ornate are the thousands of surviving work-oriented books: texts for study in universities, or manuals for parish priests at their pastoral care, books of law, medicine, and work Bibles. These were often copied in smaller—sometimes cursive—handwriting, without any adornment. To such work books were often attached, especially from the 13th century, indices and thematic retrieval systems to facilitate use, systems we still appreciate today. They combined colour markings of chapter headings—called rubrics, since they were often marked in red ink—with the arrangement of commentaries and glosses on the margins of pages. It is interesting to observe how some of these aids have been translated digitally to our screens.

The production of books was laborious, parchment and inks were expensive—a small working Bible of *c*.1300 required parchment from some 35 animals—and so only limited social and professional groups could hope to own them. Books were so precious that owners bequeathed them in wills, and passed them on within families. They were particularly costly when they contained illuminations and drawings, as so many books for religious use did. Demand for books by informed lay people as well as by the professional religious encouraged craftsmen to develop efficient methods of reproduction. The silversmiths— experts in engraving of fine metals—led the way. Johann Gutenberg (1395–1468) was a goldsmith from the city of Mainz, an entrepreneur who experimented in many innovative ventures associated with the religious culture of his day. None was more momentous than his invention of moveable type for the printing of texts. He printed the first Bible in 1455.

The rest is history.

Song

Out of the blend of traditions—Latin and vernacular, religious and secular, north and south, two ambitious cycles of poetry written in the 14th century have made their way into the canon of great world literature. They are each the result of the interaction of a poet's vision with a vast array of literary, theological, political, and scientific knowledge accumulated over the centuries we are studying. Both were ambitious projects, and each is considered as the moment when their language was perfected as a medium for literary expression—Tuscan and English—they are Dante Alighieri's (*c.*1265–1321) *Divine Comedy*, and Geoffrey Chaucer's (*c.*1343–1400) *Canterbury Tales*. Both poem cycles are organized around a journey: the former is Dante's way through Hell, Purgatory, and on to Paradise accompanied by the poet Virgil; Chaucer's is that of a group of pilgrims making their way from Southwark to the shrine of St Thomas Becket at Canterbury. Each in its way is a meditation on human worth and frailty, on the power of exemplary figures to inspire and elevate.

Poets in our period were heirs to several traditions. From antiquity they inherited the ambitious epics of war, love, and power, the greatest of all being Virgil's *Aeneid*, known to every child schooled in Latin; the Bible taught the rich structure and imagery of the Psalms, poetry which formed the daily liturgy of all religious and many engaged lay people. Traditions of oral poetry intersected with the classical and biblical all over Europe, and particularly powerfully in Iceland, Ireland, and Wales. Al-Andalus produced an exquisite culture of poetry in Arabic, whose sounds and rhythms in turn inspired the fine Hebrew poetry of Judah ha-Levi (c.1075–1141), and influenced the music of the Occitan troubadours. Traditions of epic poetry recounted deeds of heroism, like the *Chanson de Roland*, in the vernacular, and for the delight of aristocratic audiences.

The region between France and Spain—Occitania—set the tone for poetry and song from the early-12th century, and remained a point of reference for much later poetry. Poetry and music were combined and their subject was love. Human feeling, human thought, and human voice came together in the work of the Troubadours, men and women who sang love in all its pain and yearning. European love song has remained alive in European culture—later in world culture—for some one thousand years. It was produced by amateurs and professionals, by men and women, and lived both on the written page and in performance: the singer and the song, like Dylan and Baez, *trubadour* and *trobairitz*.

At the same time, Europe's religious lore was translated from Latin into vernacular languages with the aim of enriching the life of the laity. The miracles of the Virgin Mary, lovingly collected in Latin by English monks in the 12th century, were translated in the next century into the languages of England, Provence, Castile, northern France, and later on into Icelandic, Hungarian and were turned into song.

Nurtured in the courts of counts and dukes of southern France, areas that had been in constant contact with Muslim Spain, a world of warfare, lordship, and separation, songs of yearning achieved an extraordinary blend of word and sound. Somewhat later in northern France and England, songs were written by men with a Latin education, and convey a mixture of exaltation and objectification of women. This developed into the cultural style of courtly love, in which women were objects of desire, fought over by men: distant, even cruel. In the world of court and song, women were prominent patrons and promoters of love-song. Courtly love was imaginary and aspirational, but it influenced some patterns of interaction between men and women, in the etiquette of wooing and romance, which still reverberates in many genres of modern culture.

Poetry and song became attached to the rich legacy of heroic tale, which coalesced around the figure of the Briton, King Arthur, and which spread throughout Europe into all its languages. Arising from the heightened awareness of origins and ethnicity engendered by the Norman Conquest of England, in that most multi-ethnic land, the British traditions were rewritten as history. Geoffrey of Monmouth's (*c*.1100–*c*.1155) *History of the Kings of Britain*, based on Welsh and Latin sources, created a historical narrative from the Trojans who settled in Britain after the war in Troy, through complex lineages to the time of King Arthur.

Courts inspired life styles, religious and cultural trends, and influenced manners. Courts were also hubs for the production and display of luxury goods and of literature, especially the poetry which was recited and performed, sometimes sung, for the entertainment of audiences of men and women. Courts began to play at Arthurian legend, to emulate the competition, sociability, love-sickness, and gender roles this depicted. People began to take the names of Arthurian celebrities—Arthur, Lancelot, Guinevere—and to design jousts and festivities around them.

Such playfulness was the privilege of European elites for centuries, and in the 20th century it inspired a global playground. The courtly song of medieval romance provides the language of courtship, yearning, self-understanding for the world's youth. It now also fills large spaces of the imagination through role-play, games, literature, and film.

Now you know how it came about.

References

Chapter 2: People and their life-styles

For Rather of Verona: *Opera minora* (*Minor works*), ed. Peter L. D. Reid (Turnhout: Brepols, 1976), 5; and the Irish poem: *Early Irish Satire*, ed. Roisin McLaughlin (Dublin: Dublin Institute for Advanced Studies, School of Celtic Studies, 2008), 149.

On Osbert of Clare: Jacqueline Murray, 'One Flesh, Two Sexes, Three Genders?', in Lisa M. Bitel and Felice Lifshitz (eds.), *Gender and Christianity in Medieval Europe: New Perspectives* (Philadelphia: University of Pennsylvania Press, 2008), 52–75, at p. 43; on Catherine of Siena, Raymond of Capua, *The Life of St. Catherine of Siena*, trans. George Lamb (London: Harvill Press, 1960), 61.

On Hartmann von Aue: Elizabeth Archibald, *Incest and the Medieval Imagination* (Oxford: Clarendon Press, 2001), 111–13.

On Life of St Gellert: Gabor Klaniczay, '"Popular Culture" in Medieval Hagiography and in Recent Historiography', in Paolo Golinelli (ed.), *Agiografia e culture popolari. Hagiography and Popular Culture. In ricordo di Pietro Boglioni* (Bologna: CLUEB, 2012), 7–44, at pp. 17–18.

For Ingatestone, Essex: Judith M. Bennett, *Ale, Beer, and Brewsters: Women's Work in a Changing World, 1300–1600* (New York: Oxford University Press, 1996), 159; and on Floreta d'Ays: Monica H. Green and Daniel Lord Smail, 'The Trial of Floreta d'Ays (1403): Jews, Christians, and Obstetrics in Later Medieval Marseille', *Journal of Medieval History* 34 (2008), 185–211.

For the Irish poem: *Early Irish Satire*, 4; on Genovefa: Lisa M. Bitel, *Landscape with Two Saints: How Genovefa of Paris and Brigit of*

Kildare Built Christianity in Barbarian Europe (Oxford: Oxford University Press, 2009), 55–7.

On the Life of Barbatus: Paolo Squatriti, *Landscape and Change in Early Medieval Italy: Chestnuts, Economy, and Culture* (Cambridge: Cambridge University Press, 2013), 1–3.

On King Olaf: Stephen A. Mitchell, *Witchcraft and Magic in the Nordic Middle Ages* (Philadelphia: University of Pennsylvania Press, 2011), 92–3.

Chapter 3: The big idea: Christian salvation

On the Conversion of the Livs: Alan V. Murray 'Henry the Interpreter: Language, Orality and Communication in the Thirteenth-Century Livonian Mission', in *Crusading and Chronicle Writing on the Medievel Baltic Frontier: A Companion to the Chronicle of Henry of Livonia*, ed. Marek Tamn, Linda Kaljundi and Carsten Selch Jensen (Farnham: Ashgate, 2011), pp. 107–34. at 107–108.

On Dhuoda: Janet L. Nelson, 'Dhuoda on Dreams', in Conrad Leyser and Lesley Smith (eds.), *Motherhood, Religion, and Society in Medieval Europe, 400–1400: Essays Presented to Henrietta Leyser* (Farnham: Ashgate, 2011), 41–54.

On the Life of St Leoba: *Anchoress and Abbess in Ninth-Century Saxony: The Lives of Liutbirga of Wendhausen and Hathumoda of Gandersheim*, trans. with an introduction by Frederick S. Paxton, (Washington (DC): Catholic University Press, 2009), 43.

On Kołbacz: Emilia Jamroziak, *Survival and Success on Medieval Borders: Cistercian Houses in Medieval Scotland and Pomerania from the Twelfth to the Late Fourteenth Century* (Turnhout: Brepols, 2011), 85; on Løgum: James France, *Separate but Equal: Cistercian Lay Brothers, 1120–1350* (Collegeville (MN): Liturgical Press, 2012), 4; on Hathumoda: *Anchoress and Abbess in Ninth-Century Saxony*, 69.

On the *Salve regina*: Caesarius of Heisterbach, *The Dialogue on Miracles*, trans. H. von E. Scott and C. C. Swinton Bland, with an introduction by G. G. Coulton (London: G. Routledge and Sons, 1929), 497–8.

On Franciscans in Denmark: Hans Krongaard Kristensen, *The Franciscan Friary of Svendborg* (Svendborg: Svendborg County Museum, 1994), 11.

Chapter 4: Kingship, lordship, and government

On the terms and treaties: Jenny Benham, 'Law or Treaty? Defining the Edge of Legal Studies in the Early and High Medieval Periods', *Historical Research* 86 (2013), 487–97; at p. 495.

Chapter 5: Exchange, environments, and resources

On woodland: Squatriti, *Landscape and Change in Early Medieval Italy*.

On water supply: Paolo Squatriti, *Water and Society in Early Medieval Italy, AD 400–1000* (Cambridge: Cambridge University Press, 2009).

For the image of a boy fallen into a river, British Library Yates Thompson 47, fo. 94v, 1461–c.1475.

On salmon in Iceland: Steinar Imsen (ed.), *The Norwegian Domination and the Norse World, c.1100–c.1400* (Trondheim: Tapir Academic Press, 2010), 128.

Chapter 6: The 'Middle Ages' of 'others'

On Hrabanus Maurus: Julia M. H. Smith, *Europe after Rome: A New Cultural History 500–1000* (Oxford: Oxford University Press, 2005), 232.

On Geza: Smith, *Europe after Rome*, 235.

Chapter 7: The 'Middle Ages' in our daily lives

On the University of Paris: Ian P. Wei and Adam R. Nelson (eds.), *The Global University: Past, Present, and Future Perspectives* (New York: Palgrave Macmillan, 2012), 133–51, at p. 135.

On Occitan poetry: Sarah Kay, *Parrots and Nightingales: Troubadour Quotations and the Development of European Poetry* (Philadelphia (PA): University of Pennsylvania Press, 2013), 57.

Further reading

Here are some of the books that have influenced the ways we think about the period 500–1500, with their research findings and interpretations.

Marc Bloch, *Feudal Society* (London: Routledge and Kegan Paul, 1961).
Jacques Le Goff, *Medieval Civilization, 400–1500*, trans. Julia Barrow (Oxford: Basil Blackwell, 1988).
Henri Pirenne, *Medieval Cities: Their Origins and the Revival of Trade*, trans. Frank D. Halsey (Princeton (NJ): Princeton University Press, 1969).
Eileen Power, *Medieval People* (London: Methuen, 1924).
Richard W. Southern, *The Making of the Middle Ages* (London: Hutchinson's University Library, 1953).

Chapter 1: 'The Middle Ages'?

Robert Bartlett, *The Making of Europe: Conquest, Colonization and Cultural Change, 950–1350* (London: Penguin, 1994).
Nora Berend (ed.), *Christianization and the Rise of Christian Monarchy: Scandinavia, Central Europe and Rus' c.900–1200* (Cambridge: Cambridge University Press, 2010).
Michael Camille, *The Gargoyles of Notre-Dame: Medievalism and the Monsters of Modernity* (Chicago: University of Chicago Press, 2009).
Yitzhak Hen, *Roman Barbarians: The Royal Court and Culture in the Early Medieval West* (Basingstoke: Palgrave Macmillan, 2007).
William C. Jordan, *Europe in the High Middle Ages* (London: Allen Lane, 2001).

Jonathan Riley-Smith, *The First Crusade and the Idea of Crusading* (London: Athlone, 1993).

Julia M. H. Smith, *Europe after Rome: A New Cultural History 500–1000* (Oxford: Oxford University Press, 2005).

Chris Wickham, *The Inheritance of Rome: A History of Europe from 400 to 1000* (London: Alan Lane, 2009).

Chapter 2: People and their life-styles

Joan Cadden, *Meanings of Sex Difference in the Middle Ages: Medicine, Science, and Culture* (Cambridge: Cambridge University Press, 1993).

Heinrich Fichtenau, *Living in the Tenth Century: Mentalities and Social Orders*, trans. Patrick J. Geary (Chicago: University of Chicago Press, 1991).

Paul Freedman, *Images of the Medieval Peasant* (Stanford (CA): Stanford University Press, 1999).

Maurice Keen, *Chivalry* (New Haven (CN): Yale Nota Bene, 2005).

Phillipp R. Schofield, *Peasant and Community in Medieval England, 1200–1500* (Basingstoke: Palgrave Macmillan, 2003).

Chapter 3: The big idea: Christian salvation

Paul Binski, *Becket's Crown: Art and Imagination in Gothic England, 1170–1300* (New Haven (CN): Yale University Press, 2004).

Peter Brown, *The Rise of Western Christendom: Triumph and Diversity, A.D. 200–1000*, 10th anniversary rev. edn (Chichester: Wiley-Blackwell, 2013).

Caroline Walker Bynum, *Holy Feast and Holy Fast: The Religious Significance of Food to Medieval Women* (Berkeley (CA): University of California Press, 1987).

Patrick Geary, *Living with the Dead in the Middle Ages* (Ithaca (NY): Cornell University Press, 1994).

Jacques Le Goff, *The Birth of Purgatory*, trans. Arthur Goldhammer (Aldershot: Scolar, 1990).

Chapter 4: Kingship, lordship, and government

Sverre Bagge, *From Viking Stronghold to Christian Kingdom: State Formation in Norway, c.900–1350* (Copenhagen: University of Copenhagen Press, 2010).

Thomas N. Bisson, *The Crisis of the Twelfth Century: Power, Lordship, and the Origins of European Government* (Princeton (NJ): Princeton University Press, 2009).

Susan Reynolds, *Fiefs and Vassals: The Medieval Evidence Reinterpreted* (Oxford: Oxford University Press, 1994).

John Watts, *The Making of Polities: Europe, 1300–1500* (Cambridge: Cambridge University Press, 2009).

Chapter 5: Exchange, environments, and resources

Olivia Remie Constable, *Housing the Stranger in the Mediterranean World: Lodging, Trade, and Travel in Late Antiquity and the Middle Ages* (Cambridge: Cambridge University Press, 2003).

William C. Jordan, *The Great Famine: Northern Europe in the Early Fourteenth Century* (Princeton (NJ): Princeton University Press: 1996).

Paolo Squatriti, *Water and Society in Early Medieval Italy* (Cambridge: Cambridge University Press, 1998).

Chapter 6: The 'Middle Ages' of 'others'

Anna Sapir Abulafia, *Christian–Jewish Relations, 1000–1300: Jews in the Service of Medieval Christendom* (Harlow: Pearson Longman, 2011).

Dominique Iogna-Prat, *Order and Exclusion: Cluny and Christendom Face Heresy, Judaism, and Islam (1000–1150)*, trans. Graham Robert Edwards (Ithaca (NY): Cornell Univesrity Press, 2002).

R. I. Moore, *The Formation of a Persecuting Society: Authority and Deviance in Western Europe 950–1250*, 2nd edn (Oxford: Blackwell, 2007).

David Nirenberg, *Communities of Violence: Persecution of Minorities in the Middle Ages* (Princeton (NJ): Princeton University Press, 1996).

Chapter 7: The 'Middle Ages' in our daily lives

Christopher de Hamel, *Bibles: An Illustrated History from Papyrus to Print* (Oxford: Bodleian Library, 2011).

Christopher Page, *Discarding Images: Reflections on Music and Culture in Medieval France* (Oxford: Clarendon, 1993).

Ian Wei, *Intellectual Culture in Medieval Paris: Theologians and the University c.1100–1300* (Cambridge: Cambridge University Press, 2012).

Index

Expand your collection of
VERY SHORT INTRODUCTIONS